SUCCESS MINDSETS

SUCCESS
MINDSETS

Your Keys to Unlocking
Greater Success in Your
Life, Work, & Leadership

RYAN GOTTFREDSON

NEW YORK

LONDON • NASHVILLE • MELBOURNE • VANCOUVER

SUCCESS MINDSETS
Your Keys to Unlocking Greater Success
in Your Life, Work, & Leadership

Published in New York, New York, by Morgan James Publishing. Morgan James is a trademark of Morgan James, LLC. www.MorganJamesPublishing.com

ISBN 978-1-64279-691-9 paperback
ISBN 978-1-64279-692-6 eBook
Library of Congress Control Number: 2019943846

Morgan James is a proud partner of Habitat for Humanity Peninsula
and Greater Williamsburg. Partners in building since 2006.

Get involved today! Visit
www.MorganJamesBuilds.com

TABLE OF CONTENTS

PART I

WHAT ARE MINDSETS?

Chapter 1

IS YOUR THINKING
THE BEST WAY TO THINK?

Once the soul awakens, the search begins and you can never go back. From then on, you are inflamed with a special longing that will never again let you linger in the lowlands of complacency and partial fulfillment. The eternal makes you urgent. You are loath to let compromise or the threat of danger hold you back from striving toward the summit of fulfillment.
—John O'Donohue

What if you could know yourself at your deepest level? What if you could more fully awaken to how you see the world, why you possess the values and beliefs you have, why you have selected the goals you have set, and why you operate the way you do? Wouldn't you be able to navigate your life, work, and leadership more successfully?

This book is going to be a self-awakening journey. You are going to explore your deepest and most fundamental levels. While it may not always be pretty (I know from personal experience), you will become empowered to make the foundational changes required to cut your self-restraining mindsets and soar to new levels of success and your fullest potential. Are you

3

ready to explore and awaken with the purpose of reshaping and restarting your life?

Setting Off on Your Self-Awakening Journey

Let's start with this question: Do you think that your thinking is the best way to think?

My guess is that you do think that your thinking is the best way to think. If you didn't think that, you would likely change your thinking.

When you think that your thinking is the best way to think, you are preventing yourself from navigating life more successfully, excelling more fully at work, and being a more effective leader.

As a leadership researcher and consultant, I see this all the time. I regularly observe leaders, managers, and employees doing what they think is best. But commonly, for many of these people, what they think of as their best is actually dysfunctional or at least limits their potential for greater success for themselves, those they lead, and their organization.

My observations are validated by rather dismal leadership statistics:

- 44% of employees report that their current managers do not help them be more productive.
- 60% of employees report that their managers damage their self-esteem.
- 65% of employees would prefer to have a different manager compared to more pay.
- 82% of employees do not trust their manager to tell the truth.

The unfortunate reality is that the majority of employees are not managed in a way that brings out their best. This isn't because leaders aren't trying to do a good job, and it isn't because leaders are purposely being jerks to those whom they lead. It is because the way in which they see, think about, and process their world directs them to behave in a manner they think is best but is actually subpar. They are like a venturer using a faulty compass. Despite their best intentions and efforts, their inner compass's limitations prevent them from taking the best course, causing them to end up pursuing a less-than-ideal direction.

Meet Alan

Alan is the president of a nonprofit organization that primarily helps underprivileged individuals enhance themselves and their careers. Alan is well qualified to be the leader of this organization. He has worked in the industry for over 20 years and has a PhD in organizational psychology. He has taught leadership classes at a local university and a primary aspect of his job is to conduct leadership and personal development trainings.

Like most people, when I first met Alan I was really captivated by him. I already knew of his impressive background, but what really won me over was his confidence and charisma. Alan looks and talks like a stereotypical great leader. He also has a great ability to effectively articulate the importance and value of his organization, which motivates others to buy into and support his organization's cause. These traits have fueled double-digit growth in donations and revenues every year during his tenure and continue to fuel his ability to attract donors and employees to support and work for his organization.

To the external world, everything about the organization seems to be great. He seems to be getting results. But internally, things seem to be falling apart, largely because of Alan's leadership and management. All of Alan's employees are frustrated with their jobs and disengaged, and there has been a very high employee turnover rate among his employees.

Let me give you some specific examples of this discord.

First, in one instance, Alan told his employees the wrong due date for a deliverable for one of their top clients. When the client expressed frustration about not receiving the deliverable on time, Alan placed the blame on his employees.

Second, on a whim, Alan decided he wanted to roll out a new coaching service and haphazardly set a price point for the service. After hearing about the price, Taylor, the employee who would be in charge of selling the service, expressed her concerns about the price being too high. Based upon prior conversations with clients about similar products, she was under the impression that it would be really difficult to sell. Further, she was concerned that if they did sell at that particular price point, they would put the organization's reputation on the line because they would be charging a premium price on an unproven service.

Until some kinks were worked out, she was worried that their clients would not receive the same or greater value than what they would be asked to pay. Upon expressing these concerns, Alan immediately got defensive, arguing that their time was worth that amount, making him come across as though he was more interested in his own value than the value they would actually be adding to their clients. Taylor, wanting to do what was best for the organization, suggested that Alan ask his advisory board about the price at an upcoming meeting. At the meeting, the board ended up agreeing with Taylor. But, unwilling to concede that he had been wrong and trying to prove that he was right, Alan was still unwilling to lower the price to the level the board and Taylor suggested. After the initial run of the coaching service, all participants agreed that while the service was beneficial, it was overpriced. It was a blow to their reputation in the marketplace.

Third, knowing that there was discord in Alan's organization and wanting to help the situation, I asked a few of Alan's employees about their work experience. Their perspectives were all unanimous. To them, Alan is a micromanager. He manages them in a way where he primarily seeks to catch them doing things wrong, making sure that every t is crossed and every i is dotted. This approach prevents Alan from recognizing his employees' contributions and celebrating them when they do things right. In fact, when I asked, these employees were not able to recall a time when Alan had said "thank you" to them. Alan has created a culture in which employees are more focused on avoiding his attention than attempting to stand out with exemplary performance.

Finally, Keith is a new employee who was hired to work with Alan to put together training seminars. Keith came well qualified with a recent master's degree in instructional design. After reviewing the material for an upcoming seminar, Keith was quick to identify two areas for improvement. First, the material Alan would be covering was a bit outdated, primarily focused on research that came from the 1990s. Second, Alan's approach seemed to be largely a lecture-based approach. When Keith proposed updating and upgrading the seminar with new material and the use of different forms of technology designed to enhance participant engagement, Alan dismissed Keith's proposal. He stated that he has been doing this particular training for 15 years and didn't want to go through the hassle of developing new material and learning a new way of presenting it. This was demoralizing to Keith, as he felt that his investment in his education was being undervalued.

If you worked in this environment, would you want to stay?

While Alan recognizes that turnover has been an issue, he cannot see that he is the problem. He *believes* that he is a great leader. He *believes* he is doing the very best job that he can. Given Alan's confidence, he certainly considers himself to be the hero, the one who is driving significant growth in his organization.

Not willing to take ownership for the turnover issue, he is led to believe that the problem is rooted in the organization's inability to pay higher rates. This has left him blind to his employees' perspectives, who have left primarily because of his authoritarian leadership.

Alan has not truly awakened to himself, and this is preventing him from being an effective leader. Like all other dysfunctional leaders, Alan is unaware that he possesses some common, even natural, desires that cause him to make decisions and behave in ways that, to him, seem to be the best course of action but are actually having collateral damage for those around him. Thinking himself the hero, Alan is unable to see that he is actually the villain.

The villain-inducing desires Alan unknowingly possesses include looking good, being seen as right, avoiding problems, and doing what is best for himself. Specifically:

- He threw his employees under the bus to preserve his image.
- He shut down the ideas of others in an attempt to be seen as being right.
- He micromanages in order to avoid problems.
- He selected an option that was easiest for him but not likely the best for the people his organization serves.

Like a villain, Alan is largely unaware that his non-conscious desires are shaping how he thinks, sees, and operates. He is unable to recognize that when he has a decision to make or a problem to solve, he is automatically inclined to see and value only the options that feed his self-serving desires. Further, Alan feels justified. From his perspective, he likely wonders, "Who wants to look bad, be wrong, have problems, and do something that isn't best for themselves?" He is unable to see the implications and unintended negative consequences of his ego protection.

Despite Alan's best efforts, he is now one of the statistics presented earlier. He is a manager who damages his employees' self-esteem, does not help his employees be more productive, and destroys his employees' trust in him. If asked, I imagine his employees would prefer a new manager over more pay.

Just like Alan, when we fail to awaken to our foundational desires and think that our thinking is the best way to think, we limit ourselves from being more effective and successful across all areas of our lives.

I Learned This the Hard Way

It took a painful experience for me to learn this.

I enjoy running and value my daily run as a way to get exercise, pick up my energy, burn off steam, and get out into nature. I grew up playing basketball and football and I started running on almost a daily basis since high school. Until a few years ago, this near lifetime of experience running led me to consider myself a good and expert runner. If you had asked me if I wanted to take a running class to improve my form, I would have laughed at you.

I thought that my thinking was the best way to think. And I *thought* that I was awake to my "excellent" running form.

Then, I injured my knee playing basketball, which derailed my running. It was an interesting injury, because my knee felt fine unless I ran or walked up stairs. When I did those activities, I would experience a sharp shooting pain in the back of my knee.

I went to the doctor to make sure I didn't have any structural damage, and she confirmed that the knee was fine, but I had pulled a muscle in the back of my knee that just needed time to heal. So, I didn't run for two months. Itching to get back out, I started to run about once a week. Though my knee was a little better, I still had pain when I ran.

By that point, I was getting desperate for my knee to heal so I could start running consistently again. I began going to a physical therapist and started doing extensive at-home stretching and exercises. While this lessened the pain I was experiencing going up stairs, I was still having pain in my knee while running.

My next step was to get new running shoes. I went to a running shoe store, where they fitted me for some new shoes. When I checked out at the register, the salesman asked me if I wanted to sign up for a running class they were holding in a couple of days. It was designed to help runners with their form and technique.

One part of me was offended, thinking, "Are you kidding me? I am an experienced runner. I know exactly what I am doing when it comes to running." But, being desperate to heal my knee, another part of me thought, "Maybe your running form is causing your knee pain. What have you got to lose?"

So I did something I would have laughed at several months earlier: I went to the running class. The instructor taught us the four principles to good running form: (1) run tall and relaxed, (2) contact the ground mid-foot first, (3) run at a cadence of 180 steps per minute, and (4) run with a slight forward lean. It turned out that I was not following three of the four principles.

After learning and implementing the four principles, my knee pain quickly dissipated, and I was back to running on a daily basis in no time. Additionally, by changing my running form, I am now running more efficiently, which allows me to cover greater distances than I have in the past. In fact, I recently ran my first half marathon, something I never thought I would do.

Looking back, it is clear that I was not as awake to myself as I thought. My presumption that my way was the best way was preventing me from living my life at the level I desired.

This experience led me to wonder: "What else am I asleep to and missing out on because I think that my thinking is the best way to think?"

I hope it leads you to wonder the same thing.

While you may be reluctant to see or admit it, the thing that stands between where you currently are and greater success in your life, work, and leadership is yourself—in particular, your thinking that your thinking is the best way to think. But the reality is that if you want to go from your current state to a more successful state, you must think about and see the world in new, different, and better ways. You must more fully awaken to yourself.

Let's demonstrate this by pondering how you would respond to or navigate four different situations in which you might find yourself.

What Are Your Immediate Thoughts?

Consider your immediate thoughts regarding the four situations below and how you might respond to them.

1. You face a daunting challenge, one with a chance for failure.
2. Someone (e.g., a subordinate, a child, a customer) disagrees with you.
3. You face a choice between two options. One option is more certain and involves a little reward, while the other option is less certain but involves a substantially higher reward.
4. You see a homeless person on a street corner.

It is likely that you think that you approach these situations in the most optimal way. Again, if you thought you could approach them in a better way, you would likely do so.

But people see and think about these situations in different ways, and they all think they are "right."

Let's investigate some of the different ways people might think about these situations and demonstrate how their "best" thinking can limit their success.

Let's start with facing a challenge and likely failure. Do you see challenge and failure as experiences to avoid or as opportunities from which to learn and grow?

At the beginning of a recent semester, I tried to get to know some of my new students prior to class. I introduced myself to Cynthia, who was a bit older than my typical college student. Because she was a more mature student, I figured she would have an interesting story. I asked her what she did for work. Her eyes sparkled. She told me that after floundering for years, she had just started her own business as a personal trainer and health coach. She explained her passion for health and personal fitness and closed with some positive self-talk, stating that she felt it was the perfect career path for her.

About a month later, I approached her before class and asked her how things were going with her new business. She looked dejected and replied, "It isn't going so well. I don't think it's for me."

"What makes you say that?" I asked. "You seemed so sure that this was the right path for you."

"It is harder than I thought it would be, and things aren't going very well."

She explained that it is difficult to find new clients, and because of that, she was thinking about adjusting her career path once again. I tried to encourage her by noting that it had only been a month and telling her that she should give it more time and continue trying new things to learn what works and what doesn't. But she seemed determined to throw in the towel.

This entrepreneur chose to see her challenges as an indication that her venture was not the right career path and was thus quick to give up. But it could have been possible for her to instead see those challenges as a signal to adjust and improve business operations and develop the belief that success only comes to those who are persistent, exert much effort, and overcome challenges.

Next, consider disagreement. When someone disagrees with you, do you view it as a threat and get defensive? Or do you see disagreement as an opportunity to improve your thinking and learning?

Have you ever worked for leaders who feel like they need to be in control and that their way is best? In those instances, how did the leaders respond to disagreement or suggestions for change or improvement? Like Alan, the CEO of the nonprofit, they likely saw them as personal threats and responded defensively. But there are other leaders, like Ray Dalio, the founder and former CEO of Bridgewater Associates (the largest and most successful hedge fund ever), who meet disagreement with the following attitude: "If you can…practice thoughtful disagreement, you'll radically increase your learning." We'll learn more from Ray throughout the book.

What about risk? Do you see risk as something to avoid? Or do you see risk as something you must wade through in order to achieve success?

For much of my adult life, I have operated under the premise that I would be successful as long as I did not fail. This made me proactive about avoiding risk. I earned my undergraduate and doctorate degrees without going into debt, and I never had the desire to start my own business because of the risk associated with it.

But, around the time I turned 34, I recognized that I had not accomplished many things I had envisioned for my life, and that my aversion to risk was limiting me from accomplishing my life and career goals. After realizing this, I took on debt in order to start my own consulting business, knowing that I will be more successful if I approach life seeking to win as opposed to not lose. In two short years, I have been able to work with dozens of companies, several being among the largest and most well known in the world.

Finally, what are your immediate thoughts upon seeing a homeless person on a street corner asking for assistance? Do you see that person as someone who should spend their time seeking to get a job instead of asking for money? Or do you see that person as someone doing their best?

When you see a homeless person as someone who should get a job, you are likely going to think about them in a negative and critical way and lack the desire to help them. But if you see them as someone doing their best, you are left to question what has happened in their life that has caused them to believe that asking for assistance on a street corner is the best way to live. Seeing the person in this way will cause you to be much more empathetic and lead to a greater desire to help them in some capacity.

See Differently, Operate Differently

Consider the two people in the figure below, who each see these four situations differently. Who do you think is going to be more successful in their life? Who is going to be a better employee? Who is going to be a better leader? Person A or Person B?

Consider who you would rather live with, work with, or follow.

The answer to these questions is Person B. Person B is going to be more successful across their life, work, and leadership because that person is going to be more willing to take on challenges, learn, set and accomplish goals, and interact with others in more effective ways. And, since you are reading this book, I imagine you are the type of person that would much rather live with, work with, and follow Person B.

Alan is Person A. He is someone who, while trying his best, sees and interprets challenges and failure as things to avoid, disagreement as a threat, risk

Someone who sees:		Person A		Person B
Challenges and Failure	as	Situations to avoid	or	Opportunities to learn and grow
Disagreement	as	A threat	or	Necessary for learning
Risk	as	Something to avoid	or	Necessary for obtaining rewards
Others	as	Not trying their best	or	Trying their best

as something to shy away from, and his employees as people not trying their best. These negative perspectives not only drive his desires to look good, be right, avoid failure, and do what is best for himself, but they also drive him to engage in the negative behaviors that cause his employees to be so frustrated with their work environment that they want to leave.

This demonstrates something that is both simple and profound: our ability to be successful across our life, work, and leadership is founded upon how we see the world around us. If we can awaken and see the world in its most positive light, we will make better decisions, develop more efficiently, and behave more effectively.

This personal development and self-improvement strategy is generally undervalued. Most personal development and self-improvement philosophies primarily focus on evaluating and changing individuals' behaviors. But this overlooked perspective suggests that we are going to be more effective at developing and improving ourselves by awaking to and changing what drives our behaviors: the lenses we use to view and interpret our world.

How did you interpret each of the four situations? Did you interpret them more like Person A or more like Person B?

Based upon my research with a sample of over 5,000 people, I have found that only 5% of people consistently see all four situations like Person B. So, while you may think that you are navigating life in the best way possible, the odds are that you could see and interpret your world in better ways, and that your thinking is not always the best way to think.

Awakening and Empowering

Research has found that 90% of human actions, including thinking, feeling, judging, and acting, are driven by non-conscious automated processes. Additionally, self-awareness researcher Tasha Eurich states in her TEDx Talk that 95% of us believe we are self-aware, but in reality, only 10–15% of us are actually self-aware. This led her to say, "[this] means that on a good day—on a good day—80% of us are lying to ourselves about whether we're lying to ourselves."

These statistics suggest that most of us are not fully awake to who we are, what makes us tick, our desires, and how we see and interpret our worlds. For example, until reading about the different ways to view challenge and failure, disagreement, risk, and others, had you ever given much thought to how you approach these situations and whether or not you could approach them more effectively?

The point is: if we can become more awake and conscious to who we are and what is driving the non-conscious automated processes that cause us to think and operate the way we do, we will be able to better recognize our self-limiting beliefs and success-hindering desires. Correspondingly, we will become empowered to transform and improve these beliefs and desires at a foundational level.

This approach to self-improvement has been termed the self-awareness movement or consciousness revolution.

In this book, we will dive into how we see and interpret our worlds. As we do so, I invite you to introspect at a level few ever do. This book will give you a framework that will help you dive even deeper within yourself than you ever have before. We will take a look at your foundation, the internal mechanisms that power your automated processing and drive how you behave. If you can awaken to and improve these mechanisms, you will be able to recapture a larger percentage of your conscious processing and improve your non-conscious processing to unlock greater success in your life, work, and leadership.

Let the awakening begin!

Chapter 2

MINDSETS: THE DRIVERS OF OUR THINKING, LEARNING, AND BEHAVIOR

The level of the solution is never found at the level of the problem. Knowing this, you can escape many traps that people fall into. What exists at the level of the problem? Repetitive thinking that gets nowhere. Old conditioning that keeps applying yesterday's outworn choices. Lots of obsessive thinking and stalled action. I could go on. But the relevant insight is that you have more than one level of awareness, and at a deeper level there is untapped creativity and insight.

—Deepak Chopra

Have you ever tried sunglasses with different colored lenses? Perhaps you tried on sunglasses with red lenses for a few seconds, and then swapped them out for sunglasses with yellow lenses. What happened as you swapped glasses and looked around? With red glasses, certain objects attracted your attention, particularly yellow objects. But, when you put on the yellow-lensed glasses, those same objects no longer attracted your attention. Instead, entirely new objects—particularly anything white—stood out.

Let's push this a step further. What happens if you wear the sunglasses with the yellow lenses for an extended period of time (because you mistakenly thought they looked cool)? First, your brain will adjust to this new way of seeing the world. Second, you will likely lose consciousness of the fact that you are wearing glasses with yellow lenses. Third, you will forget that you are seeing the world differently than everyone else.

Did you know that you are currently wearing unique mental lenses that shape how you see the world? These mental lenses are your mindsets. Like the glasses with the colored lenses, they dictate the information that attracts your attention. This information then dictates how you interpret your world, process information, make decisions, learn, feel, interact with the world, and even how your body physically responds to the world. Stated more formally, your mindsets are the mental lenses through which you selectively organize and encode information, which in turn orients you toward a distinct way of understanding experiences and guides you toward corresponding actions and responses.

Because you wear your mindsets 24/7, you are largely not conscious of your mindsets and the impact they have on how you live, work, and lead. Yet, these mindsets are directing your life, driving much of the 90% of the non-conscious automated processing that powers your thinking, learning, and behavior.

Mindsets are the reason why different people can find themselves in the same situation and interpret that situation differently. Specifically, they are the reason why (1) some people see challenges and failure as things to avoid, while others see them as opportunities to learn and grow; (2) some people see disagreement as a threat, while others see disagreement as being an opportunity to improve one's thinking; (3) some people see risk as something to avoid, while others see risk as being necessary for success; and (4) some people see those they associate with as objects, while others see those they associate with as people. They are what leads you to believe that your thinking is the best way to think.

To demonstrate the foundational and largely non-conscious role our mindsets play in our lives, researchers Gavin Kilduff and Adam Galinsky had three groups. The first group was asked to write two paragraphs about their goals and aspirations, bringing out a goal-oriented mindset. The second group was asked to write two paragraphs about their duties and obligations, bringing out a play-it-safe mindset. The third group was a control group and did not do either writing exercise. Then, they divided participants into teams of three: one member from each group. They asked these small teams to complete a task, tracked how proactive they were in their group conversations, and then had the group members rate the reputations of the other members. They found that those with goal-oriented mindsets were more proactive in their group's discussion and viewed more favorably by their group members.

Isn't that incredible? A small task, writing just two paragraphs, imperceptibly changed the participant's mindsets, which started a chain reaction that initially caused them to interact with their groups differently and led to them being viewed differently by their peers.

Your mindsets truly shape nearly every aspect of your life, yet you are largely unaware of them. Until picking up this book, you may not have thought about the critical role your mindsets play in your life, questioned your mindsets, or sought to improve your mindsets in an educated and informed way. You have likely gone about your life believing that how you see the world is the best way and that your way of thinking is the best way to think.

This comes with both bad and good news. Bad news first: because of your unawareness of your mindsets and inability to recognize that they can be improved, you have been living life below your potential. Now for the good news: by becoming aware of your mindsets and enhancing your ability to see how they can be improved, you can become empowered to dramatically change and improve your life.

The Foundational Role of Mindsets

To demonstrate the foundational role our mindsets play in our lives, consider the pyramid to the right.

Since our mindsets shape how we see and interpret the world around us, our mindsets are at the foundation of who we are and how we live our lives (Level 1). Because our mindsets dictate how

we see and interpret our world, they drive our thinking, learning, and behavior (Level 2). Our thinking, learning, and behavior then dictate how successful we are across our life, work, and leadership (Level 3), which is ultimately founded upon our mindsets.

We can apply this knowledge in a couple of different ways. First, it helps us understand that by improving our mindsets, we can improve our thinking, learning, and behavior and thus our success across our life, work, and leadership. Second, referencing the Deepak Chopra quote at the beginning of this chapter: "The level of the solution is never found at the level of the problem." So, this pyramid suggests that if our current thinking, learning, and behaviors are not generating the success we want, we need to shift our focus from "fixing" or changing our thinking, learning, and behaviors to the level below: our mindsets.

The Power of Mindsets

Mindsets have been researched for over 30 years by psychology, management, education, and marketing scholars. Across all of this research, these scholars have repeatedly confirmed the pyramid above. Let me demonstrate this through a couple of other mind-blowing studies.

In one study, mindset research pioneers Carol Diener and Carol Dweck investigated how mindsets influence people's responses to failure. Research participants were given a mindset assessment designed to identify those with more of a negative mindset (they saw their success and failures as being caused by their ability, rather than their efforts) from those with a more positive mindset (they saw their success and failures as being caused by their efforts, rather than their ability). Then, they put the participants through an exercise where they went from having success to failing. Specifically, they gave an exam designed for the participants to get the first eight questions right and the last four questions wrong. While the students took the exam, the researchers noted the behavior of the students (e.g., did they stick with sound problem-solving strategies?) and had the students verbalize what they were thinking.

After all the participants had taken the exam, they compared the participants with more negative mindsets to participants with more positive mindsets. What they found was remarkable.

The students who possessed more negative mindsets started off very strong. As they got the first eight questions right, they became quite pleased with themselves and quite confident in their abilities. But, as soon as they hit the four difficult questions and couldn't answer them correctly, they quickly denigrated themselves. They started to experience strong negative emotions and think about themselves as failures, stating: "I am not very smart," or "I never did have a good memory." Further, they quickly dropped their problem-solving strategies (e.g., only picking brown answers because they like chocolate). To compensate for their failure, some chose to talk about successes in other aspects of their life (e.g., cast as a lead role in a play) rather than focus on the challenges in front of them.

Then, after the test, these students were asked a series of questions. The experimenters found that one-third no longer believed that they could solve the eight initial problems that they got right. Further, when asked how many questions they got right and wrong, they said, on average, five right and six wrong. They underemphasized their successes and exaggerated their failures.

The positive mindset students, on the other hand, did not even consider that they were failing. Rather than giving up, they dug in more vigorously and remained confident and optimistic, saying things like "I was hoping this would be informative," "The harder it gets, the harder I try," and "Mistakes are our friend." Rather than give up, this group maintained or even improved their problem-solving strategies; a few even managed to get a difficult question right. After the test, when asked how many they got right and wrong, they were much more accurate, essentially stating that they got eight right and four wrong.

Had we not known that these two groups differed only by the mindsets they possessed, we might be inclined to think they were from different planets, as they reacted so differently from each other on the same exact task. This one study revealed that our mindsets shape all three fundamental aspects of how we operate in life and the degree to which we succeed: our thinking, learning, and behavior. Those who possessed a negative mindset thought negatively about themselves and were incorrect in their self-evaluation; they stopped applying themselves, cutting themselves off from further learning; and they literally gave up or stopped performing. Those with the positive mindsets were more accurate in their evaluation of their performance, saw the challenge as an opportunity to learn, and continued to apply themselves. Based upon these findings, it seems clear which group is going to approach and live life more successfully.

Findings like this have been replicated for decades.

In another fascinating study, a different team of researchers, including Alia Crum, Peter Salovey, and Shawn Achor, exposed employees at a financial organization to one of two three-minute videos. One group saw a video about how stress is detrimental to our health, well-being, and performance; the other group saw a video about how stress can enhance our health, well-being, and performance. Both videos presented research-based evidence for each perspective and were designed to put employees into a stress-is-bad mindset versus a stress-is-good mindset. Then the researchers tracked the employees' health (i.e., blood pressure), engagement, and performance over the next two weeks.

Incredibly, the researchers found not only that watching the short videos adjusted the employees' mindsets toward stress, but also that the employees with the stress-is-good mindset had lower blood pressure, higher engagement, and higher performance than the stress-is-bad mindset crowd. Again, these researchers found that our mindsets imperceptibly shape how we think about, respond to, and behave within our environment. Further, this study even demonstrated that our mindsets are so powerful that they can change the physiology of our bodies and how they react to our environments, which has been verified across other studies.

Mental Fuel Filters

Every second, your brain is bombarded with dozens, if not hundreds, of pieces of information. Your mindsets filter only the information they deem to be important. The information that gets filtered and subsequently processed fuels your thinking, learning, and behavior. Hence, your mindsets are your mental fuel filters.

When people find themselves confronted with failure or stress, their mindsets attune to cues suggesting that the failure or stress is negative or positive, and they think, learn, and behave accordingly.

Your mindsets are the unseen rudders that, for now, are subconsciously directing how you navigate your life. By learning about and awakening to them, you will become more conscious of your rudders and empowered to adjust them to better navigate life. In a couple of chapters, I will invite you to take a personal mindset assessment to help you awaken to your mindsets.

Chapter 3

THE POWER OF MINDSETS TO UNLOCK GREATER SUCCESS

The day came when the risk to remain tight in a bud was more painful than the risk it took to blossom.

—Anaïs Nin

When you overlook your mindsets, you limit your ability to effectively navigate life. At a surface level, being blind to your mindsets limits your ability to be self-aware, to stand apart from yourself and examine the desires, motives, and tendencies that undergird how you think and ultimately operate.

At a deeper level, consider an aspect of your life, work, or leadership where you are currently not as successful as you would like to be. Now ask yourself, "Why am I not more successful in this aspect?"

Do you blame external factors, like not having enough money, time, or resources? Do you blame the wrong internal factors, such as your intelligence, abilities, or personality? Or, do you diagnose your lack of success as being the result of not having the most ideal mindsets?

When we do not see our mindsets as being a key part of our lack of success, we generally incorrectly blame either external factors (e.g., don't have enough money, time, or resources) or the wrong internal factors (e.g., intelligence, abilities, or personality). This misdiagnosis is problematic for at least two reasons. First, blaming these factors is closer to an excuse than a solution, because we generally cannot control these factors, at least not as easily as our mindsets. Because these factors are largely outside of our control, we hide behind them as an excuse for giving up, accepting a fate of living below our potential. We fail to recognize that others with less ideal circumstances and abilities have reached the levels of success we are seeking. Second, even if we can influence or change these factors, focusing on them instead of our mindsets means that our mindsets will likely stay the same and continually prevent us from thinking, learning, and behaving in ways that will lead to greater success.

Ultimately, when we are blind to our mindsets, we put a limit on our success. But if we can awaken to our mindsets, we unleash a world of possibility.

I make you a bold promise. After reading this book and applying its principles, your life will change. You will view your life, and yourself, through new lenses. You will dramatically deepen your self-awareness. You will be able to more accurately and effectively diagnose what is holding you back from reaching your potential. And you will be empowered to unlock greater success in your life, work, and leadership.

Below are some visual depictions of how this book can help you better navigate life and empower greater success. The first figure depicts that when we are unconscious to our mindsets and overlook them in the self-improvement process, our primary means for improving our life, work, and leadership is focusing on and pulling forward our thinking, learning, or behavior. We ask ourselves, "What do I need to learn or do differently to be successful?" When we take this approach, we fail to recognize that our prevailing and foundational mindsets will create resistance against the progress we are trying to forge on the top two levels of the pyramid. Over time, and particularly when stressful situations arise, our thinking, learning, and behavior will fall back toward our prevailing mindsets.

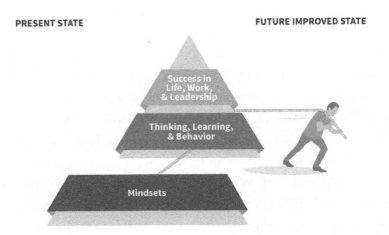

If we become conscious of our mindsets and the foundational role they play in our lives, we will approach our self-improvement in a much different, healthier, and more natural way that will lead to permanent change. This approach, depicted below, involves focusing on and pushing forward our mindsets. As our mindsets improve, naturally so will our thinking, learning, and behavior and thus our success.

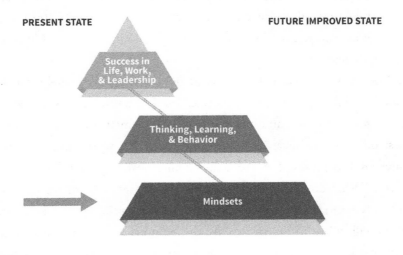

If only I had known about this sooner!

My Funk—Phase I

Have you ever been in a funk where you wanted so badly to improve your life or some aspect of your life, yet no matter what you tried to do, you did not seem to be making any progress? Maybe you are there now. Being in such a funk is not only incredibly frustrating but also demoralizing.

A few years ago, I was in such a funk. I was nearing the end of my second year as an assistant professor at California State University, Fullerton (CSUF), and several factors were causing me to question whether or not I wanted to stay. First, I wanted (and still want) my work, research, and expertise to exert a greater and more direct influence on the business community. Yet I felt that I wasn't getting enough resources or opportunities to make this impact. Specifically, I felt limited because I had very little access to funding and support that would allow me to engage in the research that would help me develop as a thought leader. While I was involved with my college's Center for Leadership, which allowed me some opportunities to do trainings for companies within the local business community, these opportunities were limited and at the mercy of the center's director.

Second, I had just received my first-year evaluations. To try to make them fair, I was evaluated by a committee made up of three members of my department as well as my department chair. My department chair gave me high marks across my research, teaching, and service. While the committee extended high marks across my research and service, they gave me the lowest possible marks for my teaching. This troubled me, because I had some of the best student evaluations in the department. In addition, I had developed a meaningful service-learning activity for my classes that allowed them to support a nonprofit that rescued children from sex trafficking, for which I would go on to win the Instructional Innovation Award from my college. While I cannot be certain, my perception was that my low evaluation for teaching was primarily driven by one member of the committee who seemed to think I was encroaching on their "territory."

The third and perhaps most significant factor in my displeasure was my perception that the future seemed darker than my present. When I was initially hired, the college offered attractive incentives that involved a sizable annual bonus of $20,000 and a reduced teaching load (two classes per semester instead of three) for the first three years. After two years of enjoying these benefits, and as I looked beyond the coming year, my perception was that my job was going to get worse (more teaching) and I was going to get paid less for doing it. Additionally, because of the high cost of living in Southern California, I had concerns about my ability to financially support my family without the bonus I had been receiving.

I felt stuck. I felt like a rocket itching to take off but restrained by my organization and some people within it.

My Funk—Phase II

Around this time, a job opening for a consulting company that I deeply respected, Gallup Inc., popped up on my LinkedIn feed. The position was for a research lead. I thought, "I love research, I love Gallup, and I don't love my situation at CSUF. Why not?" I applied and eventually took the job.

I was really excited about my new opportunity. I looked forward to having a much more direct impact on the business community by working with individual companies. I also looked forward to the opportunity to use my research skills to collect data that would drive solutions for the companies I worked with and might allow me a more direct route to become a thought leader in the business community like other or previous Gallup employees.

While I viewed this jump from academia to consulting as a permanent shift, I was encouraged by CSUF to take a leave of absence. This would allow me to go back to the university if things did not work out within a year.

When I took the job, my understanding of my position was aligned with the job description for research lead, which involved the development of research projects, facilitating data collection, analytics, and putting together reports designed to help create cutting-edge business solutions to organizations. When I went through the interview process, I was told that I would be the only one with a PhD in the Irvine office, and that many of the lead consultants would be excited to work with me, given my expertise.

When I started my role, I was first assigned to data analysis tasks across a variety of clients and projects. Although I had the expertise to do the analyses required, I do not love data analysis, particularly as a sole focus. But I was happy to do the tasks because they got me involved in projects, and it was a way to learn Gallup's structure and systems. After a few months of working solely on data analyses, I started to ask my manager for opportunities to work on projects that involved more than just data analysis and were more aligned with what I thought I had signed on for as a research lead. She tried to get me involved in projects where I could carry more than just data analyst responsibilities. While a couple of the project leads were open to this, most were not open to me contributing beyond what my role really was: a data analyst, not a "research lead."

How frustrating! I felt like I had so much more to offer than data analysis. Being one of only a few across all of Gallup with a PhD in the primary topics on which Gallup consulted, I thought I would be seen as a valuable resource to my colleagues. But, as time went on, I was given little opportunity to contribute to projects beyond data analyses. Still, I remained optimistic that I could do some job crafting.

After eight months, Gallup assigned me to a rather high-profile client. The project lead asked me to do some data analyses and present the results to the project leadership team, which involved the head of the consulting division. As I looked at the mountain of data, I asked the project lead to identify the outcomes most important for me to focus on. He told me to focus on revenues. So, I created a report around how we could help this organization drive more revenues.

Then, in the meeting, while I was presenting my findings to the project leadership team, the division head (the person I most needed to impress) questioned why I was focusing on revenues rather than profits. Being pushed up in a corner, I explained that I was told to focus specifically on revenues, somewhat throwing the project lead under the bus. Everyone in the room was frustrated.

After the meeting, the project lead pulled me aside to discuss what we could have done differently and try to figure out how to productively move forward. I suggested that I be included in the strategic conversations associated with the client. My perception was that if I had been involved in the strategic conversations from the beginning, it would have been clear to me what data the project leadership team needed. Also, being involved early would give me the opportunity to help shape the strategy of the work we were doing with the client, which was exactly the work I wanted to be doing. He replied that it would never happen, as I was only a data analyst.

I thought I was in a funk when I took my leave from CSUF. Now, I was in even more of a funk. It seemed that no matter what I tried, I was not making any progress toward my goals of having a greater and more direct influence on the business community. I felt stuck in a role that was much more narrow and much less enjoyable than I expected. Once again, I was feeling like a rocket poised to take off but restrained by my organization and the people within it.

I did not want to give up. I continued to push for more and broader opportunities within Gallup. After making little progress, my manager and I both became increasingly frustrated.

One day, after another project lead turned down my offer to contribute in a role beyond data analyst, I got on the phone with my manager and expressed my displeasure. For both her and I, the writing on the wall was clear. I was a square peg in a round hole. This position was not the right fit for me and likely would never be. She invited me to pack up my office.

I had just been let go.

My funk had just escalated to another level. While I couldn't blame my manager, it was demoralizing. It sucks to say you have been fired from an organization.

While grateful I could return to my job at CSUF, I was crushed. I felt like I was moving further away from my goals rather than closer. I had all of the tools and expertise to succeed but felt that because of the organizations I worked for and the people within, I was resigned to mediocrity.

Identifying Specific Mindsets That Drive Success

There was a silver lining, though. I had been laid off at the end of June, and my contract with CSUF didn't officially start back up until the beginning of the fall semester. This allowed me two months of freedom to jump back into my research. The project that I was most excited to revitalize was one in which we were trying to change the focus of and conversation about leadership research. The most dominant focus of leadership research for the last 70 years has been on leadership behaviors, or what leaders need to do to be effective. While this approach addresses a variety of important questions and has provided solid guidance for leaders, most believe that leadership is more than just behaviors or doing certain things. It is about *a state of being*. Yet, leadership scholars have not done a very good job of investigating the "being" elements of effective leadership.

Prior to leaving CSUF, my colleagues and I had collected data on the role that leaders' motives and focus had on their leadership effectiveness. Our preliminary studies pointed us toward the idea that leaders' motives may be as important as the leaders' actual behaviors, or perhaps even more so.

As I started to reinvestigate this idea, I continued to come across the term *mindsets* and mindset studies that cited some really interesting and powerful findings. For example, one study by Alia Crum and Ellen Langer found that when hotel workers shifted their mindsets to view daily work as exercise, over the period of a month they lost over two pounds on average compared to a group that did not believe that they got exercise from their work.

Seeing the power of mindsets, I asked myself, "If mindsets are so powerful, what mindsets do I need to have to be more successful?"

This question started me on a deep journey to identify specific mindsets that I needed to be aware of and develop. This journey took me into the academic literature across several domains, including management, psychology, education, marketing, and related literatures. From this literature review, I took away two things. First, I learned that mindsets are an individual attribute that has been studied for decades across these different literatures, and each literature seems to have focused on different types of mindsets, rarely referencing each other. In other words, these different mindsets have largely been studied in relative isolation from each other. Yet, research on each has independently reached the same conclusion: our mindsets drive our thinking, learning, and behavior. Further, the mindsets that each domain has focused on fall along a continuum ranging from negative to positive, clearly identifying mindsets that lead to more positive outcomes than their opposite counterpart.

This learning allowed me to develop something that had never been developed before: a mindset framework that united the isolated mindset literatures. I couldn't help but think that it was novel and a potentially groundbreaking way to investigate the "being" of leaders in addition to their "doings" or behaviors.

This framework is the heart of this book, and I will introduce it more fully in the next chapter.

The second thing I took away from this literature review was more profound for me personally. As I learned about these different mindsets and pieced together this framework, I couldn't help but introspect about and evaluate my own personal mindsets. As I did this, I awakened to the fact that across each of the four mindset sets, my current mindsets were largely negative. I was like Alan from Chapter 1. Within these roles, I was primarily focused on looking good, being seen as right, seeking to avoid problems, and doing what is best for myself. While I could justify these desires, I was unable to see that they actually drove me to operate in negative and self-serving ways.

As I awakened to this, it started to become more and more clear that my funk and perceived lack of success was not because of the organizations that I worked for and the people within. Rather, I had negative mindsets that were driving me to operate in ways that limited myself.

This was a humbling yet liberating realization. Humbling, because I was forced to admit that my best efforts were not the best efforts and that my thinking about my life, work, and leadership was ineffective and misaligned with my goals. Liberating, because I realized that since I was the reason for my funk, I could get myself out of it.

From there, I worked on changing my mindsets by learning more about mindsets, continuing to engage in deep-level introspection, and employing the practices that I am recommending in this book. I will readily admit that I am not perfect with my mindsets and surely have room to grow and improve, but I do believe that I have shifted them from being negative to being positive.

Looking back on my funk, I can honestly say that while it was not a pleasant experience, I am very grateful for it because of what it allowed me to learn about myself and about how to improve both personally and professionally. Without it, and without my shift in mindsets, I would not have written this book.

When I reflect upon my experience, it is clear to me that until my funk, I was blind to my mindsets. Not only was this putting a limit on my success, but it led me to think that my lack of success was the result of external factors, causing me to look for solutions to the wrong problem. The reality was that my lack of success was the result of internal factors, specifically my mindsets. And, it was not until I realized and admitted this that I was empowered to break free, opening up a world of possibility.

Opening Up Your World of Possibility

When you think about your future, what possibilities do you want to unlock?

In this book, we are going to focus on harnessing the power of mindsets to unlock possibilities and drive success in three areas: your life, your work, and your leadership.

Success in Life

What is success in life? Here are some ways to think about it:

- Success in life is not just a matter of rising to your potential but also discovering that you have more potential than you ever dreamed about.
- Success in life is having deep, loving, and mutual relationships with others.
- Success in life is learning and developing to the point that you will seamlessly do the right thing, even if it's not the easy thing.
- Success in life is having abundance to the degree that you can readily give.
- Success in life is adding value to the lives of those around us.
- Success in life is building and creating a life aligned with your dreams.

Success in Work

Regardless of where you work, whether on Wall Street, at a food pantry, or within the walls of your own home, being successful in your work means being a builder and creator of something greater than yourself. It means taking the reins as a contributor and value creator. Rather than just punching the time card or biding your time, you are actively engaged in fulfilling a mission. You are contributing in ways that add tangible (monetary, measurable) and intangible (attitude, morale, energy) value. Others hear and respect your voice, you receive recognition, and you command a salary that allows you to live with abundance. You either have security in your current job or are secure in knowing you can continually support those you are responsible for. You are, and are seen as, someone who can continue to add great value, either in a deeper way within your current position or in a new or higher-level position.

Success in Leadership

I define leadership as the ability to *positively* influence others to goal achievement. There are three aspects to this definition of leadership that I want to point out.

First is influence. For some, this word, or the idea of possessing influence, can have a negative connotation. It is helpful to remember that having influence is an important component to creating the life of our dreams and contributing to something greater than ourselves. In the words of Brendon Burchard, a dynamic speaker for the past two decades and *New York Times* best-selling author of *High Performance Habits*:

> More influence really does equal a better life. When you have more influence, your kids listen to you more. You resolve conflicts faster. You get the projects you ask for or fight for. You can get more buy-in on your ideas. You make more sales. You lead better. You're more likely to become a CEO, senior executive, or successfully self-employed. Your self-confidence goes up and so does your performance.

Second, this definition of leadership does not focus on position, level, or tenure within an organization. It only focuses on the degree to which one can positively influence others. Anyone, regardless of position, can be a leader. That's why I love Burchard's comment. An entry-level employee can bring youthful enthusiasm and energy to a stale workplace. A stay-at-home mom can create an atmosphere that allows her children to explore, develop, and rise to their potential. A largely home-bound quadriplegic can inspire his nurses, friends, and family to take full advantage of the life with which they have been blessed.

Third, this definition emphasizes the word positively. Leaders can influence others to goal achievement in either positive or negative ways. If you look back on history's most notorious leaders, they all have one thing in common: they influenced others toward achieving their dark, destructive goals, primarily through threat and force. The very best leaders do not rely upon their position, formal authority, fear, or intimidation. Rather, they influence others positively because of their qualities as a person.

Thus, at its core, being successful in leadership means that we are someone others are willing to follow and be influenced by.

Coming Up

Success across life, work, and leadership requires us to take the reins, taking full ownership of our life and destiny. Having this level of command requires that we are conscious of and in control of the very aspect of ourselves that drives essentially everything we do: our mindsets. When we take charge of our mindsets we become the driver and conscious creator of a brighter future. The alternative is settling with the mindsets life delivers to us, ultimately making us passengers and passive observers of life.

I want you to awaken to your mindsets for two reasons. By doing so, you will be able to (1) more properly diagnose and treat what is holding you back from greater success and (2) more fully take the reins of your life. Together, you will be empowered to blow past your barriers and rocket into a brighter future.

Next, I introduce you to the specific mindsets that you need to develop and improve to make this happen.

Chapter 4

DISCOVERING YOUR
CURRENT MINDSETS

You find peace not by rearranging the circumstances of your life, but by realizing who you are at the deepest level.
—Eckhart Tolle

The greatest discovery in life is self-discovery. Until you find yourself you will always be someone else. Become yourself.
—Myles Munroe

I have made the claim that our mindsets are foundational to essentially everything we do and the level of success we can reach. If this is the case, don't you think it is important that we become experts on mindsets?

Most people commonly use the term *mindsets* as part of their regular vocabulary, and they generally have a sense of their importance. When I speak to different audiences and organizations, I often ask if they know any specific mindsets that, if developed, will ultimately drive them to greater success. I generally get one of two answers: nothing (...crickets) or "a positive mindset." It is hard to disagree with "a positive mindset," but it is not a very specific answer.

Isn't this problematic?

To better understand how problematic this is, let's use an analogy dealing with our eyesight. Imagine that you are farsighted, meaning you can see things well if they are far away, but you have a difficult time seeing things close to you. Until you learn of your condition, you will accept your vision and believe that you see the world in the best way possible. Further, you will likely assume that everyone sees the world in the same way.

If you fail to recognize and admit to yourself that you have a sight limitation, you will just continue to function inefficiently (e.g., squint and hold the book you're trying to read at arm's length). You may even get frustrated about words being blurry and complain: "Why can't they use bigger type?"

Even if you recognize that you have a sight limitation and could benefit from getting glasses, if you do not know which lenses, style, or brand is best, you will be limited in your ability to improve your vision. In this state, you will essentially have two options for correcting your vision. One option is to go to a drugstore and sift through many different lens strengths and styles until you find one that corrects your vision appropriately, looks good, and is at a reasonable price. Another option is to go to see an optometrist. An optometrist will use instruments to be able to identify your current vision and tell you precisely what type of lenses you will need to correct your vision. Further, the optometrist's staff will help guide you in selecting the best-looking and best-priced glasses.

When it comes to your mindsets, our options are similar. One option is to test and try on different mindsets to see what works best. But a major problem with this is that, unlike trying on glasses in a store, our options for mindsets are not generally laid out in front of us. Most of us do not even know what options we have.

This is where I found myself when I was in my funk. I was oblivious to the importance of mindsets and assumed that my "sight" was ideal. Even when I eventually awoke to the idea that my funk was the result of my mindsets and that I needed to change them, I didn't have clarity about which of my mindsets were limiting me and which would be most optimal to possess.

To identify what mindsets I needed to have to be successful, I first turned to Google to quickly gauge the breadth of knowledge on mindsets. While

I got many hits, I was ultimately underwhelmed and disappointed because I continually found the following across the search results:

- Articles that suggested that they would discuss mindsets important for success but only talked about behaviors (e.g., create a long-term vision, listen to your gut, embrace your mistakes, take risks, be curious).
- Articles that identified different mindsets but did not clearly define what they were.
- Articles that identified and defined mindsets but did not provide any evidence that the mindset actually impacted thinking, learning, and/or behavior.

When I realized Google wasn't going to give me clear answers, I turned to the academic literature with a defined purpose: to find specific mindsets that have been repeatedly proven to influence how individuals think, learn, and/or behave. I cast a wide net across multiple fields of study. My search originally turned up about a dozen different mindsets or sets of mindsets.

There was a clear divide across these mindsets. Most of them amounted to recent developments either with no empirical support demonstrating that they affect individual's thinking, learning, and behavior or lacking enough support for me to be fully confident in their importance and value. A couple of examples include global and entrepreneurial mindsets. But there were three sets of mindsets that have been studied for decades, each largely being studied in different domains and isolated from one another: fixed and growth mindsets, open and closed mindsets, and prevention and promotion mindsets.

This left me with three sets that I could be confident were influencing individuals' thinking, learning, and behavior.

I didn't stop there. As an avid reader of any and all material concerning leadership, I was aware of a niche consulting group—the Arbinger Institute—that had published a few books on mindsets. From their works, and through personal communication, I learned that, for decades, they have been helping individuals and organizations change their thinking, learning, behavior, and success through a focus on a particular set of mindsets: inward and outward mindsets.

Bringing these four isolated sets of mindsets together has allowed me to create and present the most comprehensive framework of mindsets to date. Because each of these sets has been demonstrated to influence how effectively individuals navigate their circumstances and lives for decades, we can be confident that focusing on these particular mindsets will lead to us think and operate more successfully in our lives.

This framework provides us with an option for improving our mindsets that has not been available before. Going back to the eyesight example, this framework provides clarity on what mindset options are available to us. Not only does this enhance our ability to "shop" for better mindsets, but by creating an instrument to assess our mindsets, we can create an option similar to a farsighted person going to an optometrist, with this latter option being much more precise and effective than "trying on" mindsets until we find one that seems to feel right.

I have developed a personal mindset assessment designed to help you identify your current mindsets and the mindsets that will be more optimal for you to develop. Between this assessment and the content in this book, you should be empowered to improve how you see and operate in your world, just like a farsighted person who gets fitted with new prescription glasses after going to an optometrist.

Four Sets of Mindsets

Each pair of mindsets has a negative and a positive orientation. Being pairs, they are typically exhibited and discussed as a dichotomy, but in reality, they represent a continuum ranging from negative to positive. Think of a spectrum or shades of gray, not black or white. These sets—fixed/growth mindsets, open/closed mindsets, prevention/promotion mindsets, and inward/outward mindsets—are presented with their continuum nature in the figure below.

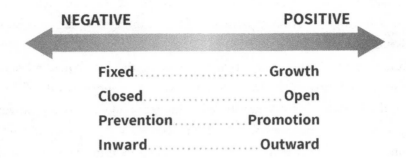

This figure and supporting research show that individuals' mindsets lie somewhere along each of the four continuums. Regardless of where we are along the continuum, if we can improve our mindsets and make them more positive, we will naturally and effectively improve our thinking, learning, and behavior and, by doing so, enhance our success in life, work, and leadership.

Since the four positive mindsets on the right side of the figure (growth, open, promotion, and outward) have been repeatedly found to result in navigating life more effectively and successfully, I will refer to them as Success Mindsets. They are the keys to unlocking greater success in our life, work, and leadership. The four negative mindsets on the left side of the figure (fixed, closed, prevention, and inward), while easy to justify, have been consistently found to prevent and limit success. Thus, I will refer to them as Limiting Mindsets.

Invitation to Take a Personal Mindset Assessment

While we have identified the mindsets that we will focus on for the remainder of this book, I will refrain from defining and describing them now. I do this because if I prematurely define and explain these mindsets before you take the personal mindset assessment, it may prevent you from answering questions in the mindset assessment as honestly and accurately as possible, thus biasing your results.

I invite you to now take your personal mindset assessment. I encourage you to answer as honestly as possible. Focus on answering from your current mindset, not how you would ideally like to answer. You will gain little value in the assessment if you are not honest with yourself.

Also, it is not uncommon for us to have certain mindsets in one environment (e.g., work) and slightly different mindsets in a different environment (e.g., home). So, as you take the assessment, think about the environment where you spend the most time or energy or the environment that means the most to you.

The assessment takes approximately seven minutes. For each question, you will be presented with two polarizing statements. Select the degree to which you feel like each is an accurate depiction of who you are.

Once you answer all of the questions, an individualized and comprehensive report will be sent to the email address you provide. The report will contain information to help you:

- Better understand each of the four sets of mindsets.
- Identify where your mindsets stand along each of the four mindset continuums. (Specifically, you will get a score for each set of mindsets, along with a ranking of where you stand relative to others who have completed the assessment.)
- Improve your mindsets.

To take the assessment, visit
https://www.ryangottfredson.com/successmindsets.

Many people who take this assessment call it a life-changing or an organization-changing experience. To give you some examples, multiple recently divorced individuals have taken the assessment and told me that if they had awakened to their mindsets earlier, they would have seen a clearer way to improve their marriage and probably wouldn't have gotten a divorce. Those experiences are both humbling and sad as I consider both the perceived value of the assessment and the massive what-ifs.

Dozens of organizations ranging from Fortune 10 to midsize companies have used the assessment to develop their top leaders. Human resource leaders have told me that executives are unconsciously being the villains in their organization, and they need a tool and training to help them awaken to their villainy. Unfortunately, such situations are not uncommon. Travis Bradberry and

Jean Greaves, in their book *Emotional Intelligence 2.0*, report that top executives generally have the lowest levels of emotional intelligence in their organizations. Acknowledging this, it is not surprising that executives are not always receptive to taking a mindset assessment and going through a training. But when they do, it is hard for them to deny the objectivity of the mindset assessment as their mindsets are compared to thousands of others. This objectivity generally awakens them enough to enhance their self-awareness and emotional intelligence.

Just as this assessment has been an awakening moment for others, it will be an awakening moment for you. It will help you see yourself in a new way.

If you happen to possess any Limiting Mindsets, do not beat yourself up. Receiving your results represents a starting place. We shouldn't expect to be great at something we have never really focused on. If you possess any of the Success Mindsets, such results will help you to have greater confidence in yourself. Regardless of your personal results, making improvements across your mindsets will enhance your success.

The assessment is a barometer for your mindsets. You can come back to it at any time to observe the changes and progress you are making.

The Power of Labels

A primary reason why this mindset framework has the power to enhance your self-awareness and success is because it assigns clear labels and definitions to your mindsets. Without these labels and definitions, it is difficult, if not impossible, to have clarity and precision on what to focus on when attempting to upgrade your mindsets. It is like shooting in the dark. By assigning labels, you have the clarity, direction, and power to introspect about your current mindsets and develop the four Success Mindsets.

Learning about and assigning clear labels and definitions has changed my life. When I first learned about the mindset sets, I awakened to my personal foundation, and it wasn't pretty. I became aware that my mindsets fell on the negative side of the continuums and were detrimental to my success in my life, work, and leadership. Until then, I felt right and justified in the mindsets I was wearing. I thought my way of thinking was the best way to think. I was so wrong.

By awakening to my existing mindsets and acknowledging they were not conducive to my desired success, I became empowered to change. While I am still a work in progress (aren't we all?), I feel like I am now on the positive side of each of the four continuums. As I made this shift and developed new mindsets, it has become obvious that my thinking, learning, and behaving has improved. I now feel much more confident in my ability to achieve greater success in my life, work, and leadership.

I am excited about the new opportunities and enhanced success that my new mindsets will fuel.

I want you to experience that same optimistic excitement about yourself and your future.

The Cognitive Science behind Mindsets

Before we move forward, I think it is critical that we understand exactly what our mindsets are and how they function within our brain. This understanding will help solidify their position as being foundational to everything we do and help clarify how we go about improving our mindsets.

Thus far, I have compared mindsets to mental lenses or a mental fuel filter. While these are the roles they serve, mindsets are actually the neural networks in the prefrontal cortex that are associated with associative processing memory. Let me explain.

The prefrontal cortex is the brain's executive control center. It is where information from our senses is quickly transmitted to be processed to guide thoughts, feelings, and behaviors. This is where the filtering occurs. Now, there isn't actually a filter, but the filtering effect is driven by certain neural networks that are more prone and ready to fire than others.

Neural networks comprise connections between brain cells, or neurons. Neurons have three main components: a cell body (soma), axon, and dendrites. The cell body is the part of the cell in which an electrical impulse is generated. This impulse travels to the axon, where specific chemicals called neurotransmitters (e.g., dopamine) are released into a space between neurons, called the synapse, where the axon of one neuron is closely connected to the dendrite of another. The series of neural connections make up a neural network.

Our brain has two memory systems. One is called the fast-binding system, and it rapidly records episodic memories. For example, think back on the last trip you took. Can you recall a particular experience in almost complete detail? That is your fast-binding system at work. We generally can access it only through conscious thought.

The other memory system is called the associative processing system. This is a slow-learning memory system. It uses knowledge accumulated from a large number of experiences to fill in information, quickly and automatically, about the current situation based upon similar situations we have previously experienced. In other words, when we observe a cue from one situation (e.g., this situation seems risky), our associative processing system automatically retrieves information from our prior experiences (e.g., I got burned last time I took a risk) to help us understand how to best navigate our current situation. This memory system operates largely non-consciously, and it helps us to quickly make sense of the situations we encounter.

The more we rely upon certain representations, the more we strengthen the neural connections associated with those representations within our associative processing system. What this means is that as a neural connection increases in strength, the axon will increase its ability to release neurotransmitters and the dendrite will develop more dendritic receptors to capture the neurotransmitters. Hence, certain neural connections become more prone to fire and will fire more rapidly than others.

These strong neural connections within our associative processing system are our mindsets. They largely operate automatically and non-consciously, and they cause us to quickly process information in predictable and repeated ways over time. This is why scholars estimate that 90% of our thinking, feeling, judging, and acting is driven by our non-conscious automatic processes.

Just because our brain may be more prone to fire in one way (e.g., seeing a challenge as something to avoid) does not mean we can't process in different ways (e.g., seeing a challenge as something to approach). It just means that if we want to develop more positive mindsets, we have to overcome our current wiring by engaging in more conscious thought and specific interventions designed to enhance our reliance upon the less-used but more positive neural connections.

The four sets of mindsets identified are simply specific categorizations of these different neural connections.

Moving Forward

The next four sections will dive into each of the four sets of mindsets. Each section follows the same four-chapter structure. The first will define and describe each mindset set. The second will demonstrate how the negative and positive mindsets drive our thinking, learning, and behavior. The third will demonstrate how the mindsets ultimately fuel our success in our life, work, and leadership. And the fourth will discuss how you can improve your existing mindsets.

If you haven't already, I invite you to complete your personal mindset assessment now, so we can start diving into each mindset set and awakening even more to our own mindsets.

PART II
GROWTH MINDSET

Chapter 5

DISCOVERING A GROWTH MINDSET

Why waste time proving over and over how great you are, when you could be getting better?

—Carol Dweck

The date is November 10, 2012. Texas A&M's football team is ranked 15th in the country, and they are squaring off against the top-ranked Alabama Crimson Tide, the defending national champions. Seven minutes into the game, with Texas A&M leading 7-0, the Aggies line up on Alabama's 10-yard line, threatening to score. It is third and goal. If Texas A&M can score on this play, they will go up by two touchdowns on a team that has been dominating opponents by an average of 19 points per game. If they don't score, they will have to settle for a field goal, a huge missed opportunity.

With three seconds remaining on the play clock, the ball is snapped to Johnny Manziel, a freshman quarterback whose electric play has captured the nation's attention. Manziel drops back from the shotgun, but pressure from Alabama arrives quickly. He scrambles to his right but is almost immediately cut off. As he spins away, he collides with a teammate and the ball pops up into the air. Cool as a cucumber, Manziel catches the ball, runs into open space to his left, sets his eyes downfield, and fires a gentle pass to his wide-open teammate in the back of the end zone. Texas A&M goes up two touchdowns. They go on to win the game 29-24, with Manziel completing 24 of 31 passes for 253 yards and two touchdowns. For good measure, he also rushed for 92 yards.

This came to be known as Manziel's Heisman "moment," a spectacular play in a big game that convinces Heisman Trophy voters that the player is deserving of college football's most coveted award. One month later, at season's end, Manziel indeed became the first freshman to ever win the Heisman Trophy, recognizing him as the top collegiate football player. In addition to the Heisman, he also became the first freshman to win the Manning Award and the Davey O'Brien National Quarterback Award, both recognizing him as the nation's top quarterback.

It was an incredible feat. But something else made it more incredible: Manziel essentially operated on talent alone. Proclaiming himself not to be an X's and O's guy, Manziel convinced his coaches to refrain from giving him an actual playbook. A quarterback without a playbook? Not only that, but he rarely watched film. What instinct!

Manziel was on top of the football world. With that, he quickly rose to the heights of the social world as well, frequently appearing in the news for partying with professional athletes (James Harden, Rob Gronkowski) and other pop culture stars (Justin Timberlake and Drake). He was destined to be a star.

Unfortunately, despite all of his natural talent and huge upside, this became the peak of Manziel's career.

Had Manziel been eligible to enter the NFL draft after his freshman year, he probably would have jumped in. However, NFL rules state a draft choice must be three years removed from high school. He returned to Texas A&M for one more year, where he continued to electrify the country and add to his already incredible statistics. But because of off-field issues that included a reputation for being a partier, his draft stock declined prior to the 2014 NFL draft. A leaked NFL scouting report included the following:

- Coaches "can't yell/scream at him or he shuts down; has walked away from [coach] in the past."
- "Knows how to scheme the system, arrogant and full of himself, but he's not smug to coaches. Has been like this since Day 1, has never gone to class, goes to beat of own drum, but has ultimate confidence."
- "The definition of the word maintenance. CONCERNS: Maturity, passion for preparation, high maintenance, work ethic."

At the 2014 NFL draft, the Cleveland Browns traded up to select Manziel with the 19th overall pick. When he first started working out with the team, one Browns teammate said that Manziel "dropped jaws" in practice with his athletic ability.

Sadly, that proved to be Manziel's high-water mark with the Browns. During his rookie year, he continued to think that talent alone would allow him to succeed. He put in very little effort compared to successful professional quarterbacks, who are borderline obsessive-compulsive about every detail ranging from what they eat to the exact air pressure in their footballs to the various defensive schemes their opponents employ. Manziel wasn't opening his iPad playbook on the weekends. Instead, he partied with celebrities. With such lack of preparation off the field, he struggled in practice. He later went on to say that he quickly lost confidence in his abilities, as it was the first time he had struggled on the football field since his freshman year of high school. "That's when the depression started to come," he added.

Like many rookies, Manziel didn't initially start for the Browns. But late in the season, with the Browns struggling to produce wins, they went to him to spark some wins. In his first game, he threw two interceptions, finishing with one of the lowest passer ratings possible. Not surprisingly, the Browns lost, 30-0. After the game, teammates complained that he either didn't know the plays in the huddle or didn't call them correctly. A week later, he injured his hamstring and was done for the season.

Manziel's life continued to unravel. A week after injuring his hamstring and the night before Cleveland's last game of the season, Manziel flew to Las Vegas to party. He ended up missing his flight back for mandatory treatment for his injury, severely tarnishing his image to his coaches and teammates. Over the course of the next year, he was in and out of rehab for drug- and alcohol-related problems, continued to have off-the-field and legal issues, and was eventually released by the Browns. After going through more rehab and sitting out entirely for a couple of seasons, he tried to revive his football career in the Canadian Football League. He threw four interceptions in his debut start with the Montreal Alouettes and was quickly benched. Now, at age 26, he is out of professional football after a brief try in the short-lived Alliance of American Football.

To me, what is so fascinating about Johnny Manziel's life is how he seemed to be destined for greatness, burning bright with the obvious talent to succeed. Instead, he flamed out in rather spectacular fashion.

You can probably think of other examples like this. They are everywhere: supremely talented individuals who seem like sure bets but turn into big-time washouts. Then there are individuals who do not appear to have the natural talent to succeed that proceed to do amazing things and achieve greatness. Think of Tom Brady, perhaps the greatest quarterback ever. Brady was largely a nobody when he came out of the University of Michigan, rated as a slightly above-average quarterback at best. He was drafted with a compensatory sixth-round choice, just 199th overall. Usually, players drafted at this level end up being cut as teams have to whittle down their rosters to 53 men during the preseason. If you have ever seen him play, or if you have ever watched him work out, you know that he is not as physically athletic as compared to most in the NFL, perhaps even quite slow. Yet, he's the most decorated quarterback of all time with six Super Bowl rings, nine AFC championships, four Super Bowl MVP awards, and two NFL MVP awards. And he may not be done yet.

When you look at Manziel, the first freshman to win the Heisman trophy and the 19th overall pick, and Brady, the 199th overall pick, key questions arise: What allows some people to succeed, perhaps despite their disadvantages? What causes other, often extremely capable people to fail? The answer often lies in whether they have a fixed or growth mindset.

Fixed and Growth Mindsets

When someone possesses a fixed mindset, they believe that their abilities, talents, and intelligence, as well as those of others, cannot change. When someone possesses a growth mindset, they believe that their personal attributes are able to change.

This is a small difference with huge implications. Each of us has a battle going on within. We want to look good to others, but we also want to learn and grow. However, it is quite difficult to do both at the same time. If we want to look good, we are unlikely to put ourselves in positions where we may make mistakes and fail. But aren't these the very situations where we are likely to learn and grow the most? To resolve this battle, we end up developing neural connections that cause us to focus on one over the other: looking good or learning and growing.

Those with a fixed mindset place priority on looking good. Why? The primary reason is because if someone does not feel like they can change and they fail, the only logical explanation to them is that they are a failure. Thus, at a deep and often non-conscious level, they are primarily motivated by the fear of being seen as a failure. They avoid challenges and give up easily when the going gets tough. Additionally, since they see their and others' characteristics as things that can't change, they tend to believe that you either "have it" or you don't. As such, they believe that success should come naturally and quickly, and if it doesn't, they take it as a sign that they were not meant to do it. Thus, they largely avoid exerting significant or concerted effort.

Carol Dweck, the researcher who pioneered the identification of growth and fixed mindsets, has stated that the hallmarks of a successful person are a lifelong love of learning, tendency to seek challenges, valuing effort, and persisting in the face of obstacles. Based upon the description of someone with a fixed mindset above, does it seem like a fixed mindset individual is going to possess these hallmarks?

Those with a growth mindset place priority on learning and growing. As such, they seek to put themselves in positions to maximize their development. Rather than avoiding challenges or getting frustrated when facing challenges, they see them as opportunities to advance and progress and remain optimistic.

They do not believe that success should come naturally. As such, they are much more willing to invest effort and persist beyond failure. Rather than give up when the going gets tough, they actually dig in and ramp up their effort even more. That is why some sports stars, like Tom Brady, work harder and succeed more than others with similar or greater physical talents.

The power of these mindsets was demonstrated in a study I described in Chapter 2. As you'll recall, students who took a mindset assessment were put into two groups and presented with 12 questions—eight easy and four challenging. The researchers, including Carol Dweck, found that when those with a fixed mindset began to fail, they started viewing themselves as failures. Specifically, they lost confidence in their abilities, engaged in negative self-talk, gave up, and no longer felt they had the ability to succeed. But those with a growth mindset responded much differently. They didn't believe that struggling with questions revealed anything about them personally; rather, they saw the difficult questions as an opportunity to learn and grow, so they dug in more vigorously.

Reflecting back on Johnny Manziel, what mindset did he seem to have? Did he seem to believe that success should come naturally? Did he seem to persist when the going went tough? Did he learn from failure, or did he internalize it?

It is clear that Manziel had the talent to rise to the near pinnacle of sporting success. But, it's also clear that his mindset led to his fall from the top.

Drivers of Growth and Fixed Mindsets

What leads some people to develop a fixed mindset, while others develop a growth mindset?

One factor relates to our upbringing. Research has repeatedly found that the praise we receive from our parents and teachers growing up shapes our mindsets. Specifically, praising one's abilities (e.g., "You are so smart!) sends a fixed mindset message that cements the importance of being seen as having ability, talent, and intelligence. Conversely, praising one's efforts (e.g., "You worked so hard at that!") sends a growth mindset message that emphasizes learning, growing, and developing one's abilities. Also, it appears that the degree to which we feel loved and accepted by our parents shapes our mindsets. If children feel insecure about being accepted, they feel lost and alone. In order to combat this anxiety, they seek ways to feel safe and win their parents over, often by creating or imagining other "selves" that their parents might like better. Unfortunately, these other "selves" emphasize pretending to be a certain way or possessing certain qualities, which fuels a fixed mindset.

Second, the contexts in which we live and work play a role in the mindsets we develop. Consider our education system. Does a standard grade school and high school education today emphasize learning and mastering the material? Or does it emphasize sky-high grades that look good on college transcripts? The social emphasis on getting good grades drives a fixed mindset among many, if not most, students. They become more concerned about how they look on paper than how much they learn. As I teach and work with college students, I find that when they enroll in classes, they place a premium on finding courses that will allow them to get an easy A over classes that will most help them develop as a person and professional. On this topic, Ray Dalio of Bridgewater Associates states, "I've often thought that parents and schools overemphasize the value of having the right answers all the time. It seems to me that the best students in school tend to be the worst at learning from their mistakes, because they have been conditioned to associate mistakes with failure instead of opportunity. This is a major impediment to their progress."

Work environments also influence one's mindset. Enron is a classic example. The culture of Enron placed an emphasis on talent, creating a culture of genius. Because they believed that employees either had talent or didn't, they focused more on hiring top talent than developing their employees. This created a culture that emphasized demonstrative displays of talent, looking good, and never making mistakes, and it socially incentivized leaders and employees to want to shine brighter than their peers. This ultimately led to leaders and employees taking shortcuts, hiding information, and keeping secrets, which eventually resulted in Enron's collapse and its two top leaders, Kenneth Lay and Jeffrey Skilling, being convicted of fraud.

What Mindset Do You Have?

Carol Dweck's research revealed that the population is split between possessing fixed and growth mindsets. What did the personal mindset assessment reveal about you? If you have more of a fixed mindset, do not carry it and believe that you can't change it. We *can* change our mindsets. That is the beauty of focusing on them for personal development. In fact, across studies on fixed and growth mindsets, researchers have found that very small interventions (e.g., 15-minute training, reading a few paragraphs) can improve your mindset.

Regardless of your assessment results, you will be empowered to develop more of a growth mindset as you become more aware of the differences between fixed and growth mindsets and the role they play in how you live, work, and lead.

Let's continue this process of exploration and awakening so that we can more fully develop the hallmarks of success laid out by Carol Dweck—love of learning, seeking challenges, valuing effort, and persisting in the face of obstacles.

Chapter 6

HOW GROWTH MINDSETS DRIVE THINKING, LEARNING, AND BEHAVIOR

How you think when you lose determines how long it will be until you win.
—Gilbert Keith Chesterton

C hristopher Langan has been called the smartest man in the world because, well, he may literally be exactly that. The average person has an IQ of 100. Albert Einstein had an IQ of 150. Christopher Langan's measured IQ is 195.

In our society, we're conditioned to believe that a high IQ naturally means high achievement or the ability to create something so genius, so disrupting, that it changes the world in some way, like Einstein did with his theory of relativity. Yet, what dramatic contribution has Langan made to the world? What did he win a Nobel Prize for? While the door is not closed on Christopher doing great things, thus far he has spent much of his life working as a bar bouncer in Long Island, New York.

What causes naturally gifted, intelligent people like Christopher Langan and Johnny Manziel to dramatically underperform relative to talent level and respective expectations?

To answer this question, mindset pioneers Barbara Licht and Carol Dweck initiated a study by having students take a mindset assessment to distinguish those with a fixed mindset from those with a growth mindset. Next, they instructed half of each type of students to read a workbook and answer seven questions. In this first group, 68% of the growth mindset students got all seven questions right, while 77% of the fixed mindset students answered them all correctly. Next, they asked the other fixed and growth mindset students to perform the same task, except this time, they inserted an obscure and hard-to-read paragraph on the first page. That was the only difference between the workbooks. For this second group, 72% of the growth mindset students got all seven questions right, essentially the same as the first group. Shockingly, only 35% of the fixed mindset students did the same. This led Licht and Dweck to conclude that many fixed mindset students with the necessary skills failed to learn the material and perform well because they didn't possess the cognitive flexibility to get past the initial confusion. They didn't have the mindset to deal with adversity.

When I first read this study, it made me wonder how many times I underperformed because my mindset didn't allow me to get past something minor, such as an obscure, hard-to-read paragraph.

Undoubtedly, the fixed mindset students who underperformed felt like they were trying their best, but they were left scratching their heads, wondering what went wrong. This is likely the case with people like Christopher Langan and Johnny Manziel. While they tried their best in their own minds, it is also evident their mindset caused them to think, learn, and behave in ways that now leave the general public scratching their heads, wondering how such capable and talented individuals could fail to live up to their possibilities. Sadly, in Manziel's case, it played out in the national media for years, greatly damaging his public reputation.

Let's dive more fully into the foundational role our fixed and growth mindsets play in our life by exploring how they influence our thinking, learning, and behavior.

Thinking

The core difference between those with a fixed mindset and those with a growth mindset is their belief in whether or not individuals can change and improve their talents, abilities, and intelligence. This may seem like a small difference, but it has huge implications.

Those with a fixed mindset believe that people are unable to change and see people as either having the talents, abilities, and intelligence to perform at a high level and be successful or not. This perspective causes them to be mentally programmed to non-consciously and consistently assess the degree to which they and others are succeeding or failing. Depending upon the level of performance, their fixed mindset is quick to assign a near-permanent label of some degree of "have" or "have-not."

Those with a growth mindset believe that people's talents, abilities, and intelligence can be improved, and they do not think in terms of "haves" and "have-nots." Rather, they are programmed to conclude that how one performs today and in the future has more to do with how much practice and effort they have put in previously, rather than their innate abilities.

Because of this fundamental difference, fixed and growth mindset individuals develop and possess drastically different values, priorities, and fears. Those with a fixed mindset are very concerned about their status as a "have" or "have-not." In fact, their value and sense of self-worth is derived by the degree to which they are a "have." This makes them overly concerned about their image, and they will go to great lengths to protect it. This also means that those with a fixed mindset have the underlying fear of looking bad fueling much of their thinking and processing.

Since those with a growth mindset believe that one's level of performance is more reflective of their effort than their abilities, they care much less about how they look and much more about how much they are growing, developing, and progressing. Thus, rather than focus on their image, or exterior, they focus on their development, or interior. They don't want to just look good; they want to be good. Thus, their fears revolve around not reaching their potential.

Let's pause for a moment. The differences that I have described are hugely significant. On one hand, we have those with a fixed mindset, who are programmed to look good and protect their image and possess an underlying fear of looking bad. On the other hand, we have those with a growth mindset, who are programmed to be good and improve their abilities because their underlying fear is not reaching their potential. Does one mindset seem more likely to prime one for success than another?

Once we recognize these differences, they become fairly easy to see, especially when watching sports. Consider the Golden State Warriors of the National Basketball Association (NBA). They and their all-star cast are rather recognizable, having been to the NBA finals for the last five years. One of their all-star players is Draymond Green. He is known as the "glue guy." This means that while he is not the star player, he is willing to do the little things (e.g., make great passes, set screens, and get rebounds) to make the team successful. One of the things Draymond Green is known for is complaining to the referees and getting technical fouls. Across his seven-year career, he has received 78 technical fouls. Some argue that he cost his team a championship trophy in 2016 because he got so many technical fouls during the playoffs that he was suspended for a critical game in the championship series. Also, and especially in heated moments during games, when he makes a mistake such as a bad pass, he will throw his arms up in disgust, generally at one of his teammates. Antics like this have led to publicity about conflicts between him and his teammates.

Another player for Golden State is their star point guard Steph Curry. Many consider him to be the best shooter to ever play. He is recognizable because after making a shot, he has a habit of tapping his heart and pointing to the sky. Of this, he says, "[It] basically means 'have a heart for God.' It keeps the perspective for me why I play the game and where my strength comes from…It's been a good kind of grounding." He does not believe that his success is fully because of his talents, abilities, and intelligence. After a mistake or a bad play, you rarely see him react in a negative way. If anything, you generally see him talking to himself, likely about how he can improve. Across his 10-year career, he has received only 17 technical fouls.

From an observer's perspective, it appears Draymond Green has more of a fixed mindset. He appears overly concerned about how he looks and likely has an underlying fear of looking bad. Thus, when he makes a mistake, he is mentally programmed to react negatively because he believes his mistake sends a signal that he is a "have-not," and he seeks to blame others to protect his status as a "have." Steph Curry, on the other hand, appears to have more of a growth mindset. He does not appear to see mistakes as an indicator that he is a "have-not." Instead, when he makes mistakes, he is able to view them as something to learn from, and he uses those mistakes to further develop his skills and abilities.

Each player has clearly been successful, each winning three NBA championships and being named all-stars across multiple seasons, but when we consider how effectively each operates for their own success as well as for their team's success, there seems to be a clear difference. Further, when we consider which player has the mindset to be able to enhance their skills moving forward, there also seems to be a clear difference.

Learning

Over 30-plus years studying fixed and growth mindsets, researchers have found that there are two primary reasons why those with these mindsets operate so differently and obtain different levels of success. These two reasons strongly relate to how likely they are to learn and develop and involve how they think about failure and effort.

To those with a fixed mindset, failure is kryptonite. In their mind, failure exposes them as a "have-not." To protect their image, they are non-consciously programmed to avoid failure. Since challenges are situations with the risk for failure, one's fixed mindset will also cause them to see challenges as things to avoid.

An indicator of the size of a challenge that those with a fixed mindset are sensitive to is the question "How much effort is this going to take?" If they perceive that a task will come easily to them and require little effort, they see it has having a low likelihood for failure and they become willing to take it on. But if they perceive that a task will require a high degree of effort, they will see it as having a high likelihood for failure and become inclined to avoid it.

Correspondingly, those with a fixed mindset believe that success should come naturally, and if something isn't coming naturally, it is a signal that they are a "have-not." From this perspective, when challenges or difficulties arise, they would prefer to give up and try to find success by heading in a new direction rather than by exerting significant effort on their current path.

This fear of failure and challenges and perception that effort is a sign of being a "have-not" was Johnny Manziel's primary issue. He felt like success should come naturally, and that if he was truly talented, he wouldn't need to engage in effort. In fact, seeing effort as a sign of weakness, he was unable to rise up to the challenge of becoming a great professional quarterback.

Not being concerned about being a "have," those with a growth mindset do not view failure and effort so negatively. They see failure as being incredibly valuable. To them, there is no better way to identify areas where they can enhance themselves than in an area where they failed. Thus, those with a growth mindset are programmed to welcome challenges as opportunities to push themselves and learn from their experiences.

When facing a challenge, those with a growth mindset may still ask, "How much effort is this going to take?" But they ask this not to gauge how easily the task will come to them but to determine how much they might grow because of it. Knowing that growth stems from effort and success stems from growth, when the going gets tough, they do not back away like someone with a fixed mindset is inclined to do. Instead, they become willing to exert effort in their path to success.

Again, we can ask ourselves who is going to operate more effectively. Those who see challenge and failure as things to avoid and effort as a sign of weakness? Or those who welcome challenge and failure as opportunities to learn and grow, and recognize that success requires effort?

Let me summarize with an example that strikes close to home (and don't tell my wife I told you this). When we first got married, my wife did not have much baking experience. Yet, she continually said that she wanted to learn how to bake. Unfortunately, at the time, she possessed a fixed mindset that led her to shy away from baking, because she saw it as something she would likely fail at. Her mind non-consciously connected the dots in a stereotypical fixed mindset way: if she were to fail at baking, then she would be a "failure" as a wife. Worse, she was worried her new husband would see her as such. So, for several years, she never attempted to bake. When she eventually did, it was common for her baking to not turn out right (e.g., doughy bread, flat cookies). After such failure, it would take her months to be willing to try again. Her mindset did not let her see that effort was the path to success.

In the instances when something she made flopped, I tried telling her that all she needed to do was to practice more, and that through 10 to 20 attempts, and perhaps that many failures, she would continually learn and adjust, eventually mastering the desired recipe.

Now, after a decade of marriage and much to my pleasure, I am happy to report that she slowly accumulated enough attempts to develop some accomplished baking skills, including making a tiger-striped birthday cake for our son, to-die-for banana bread, and savory cheesy garlic rolls. She now bakes on a regular basis.

This leads to a question: How much more quickly would she have learned to bake if she had awakened to and adjusted her fixed mindset sooner, making herself more open to failure and concerted effort?

In hindsight, it is easy to see the impact her fixed mindset had on her ability to learn and master a desired skill. But, in the process, she was not aware that her fixed mindset, with its associated need to look good and its corresponding fear of failure, is what stood between where she was and what she desired to accomplish. Had she become aware of her fixed mindset earlier and made some adjustments to the lenses that she viewed herself with, learning how to bake would have been much more efficient and enjoyable.

Behavior

If we see challenges and failure as things to avoid and effort as a signal of our limitations or of being on the wrong path, we are going to behave very differently than if we see challenges and failure as opportunities to learn and effort as the path to mastery.

Reflecting upon my life, I can clearly see how having a fixed mindset altered my life's path.

As early as I can remember, I had a fixed mindset toward my education. I was much more concerned about my grades than I was actually learning. As such, I always did the minimum amount to get an A, and I was able to accomplish that for nearly all my classes, earning me an academic scholarship my freshman year of college. I promptly carried this mindset with me as I went to college.

I went to college planning to become a medical doctor. This meant that I needed to take the year-long pre-med freshman chemistry course taught by the former 3M chemist who actually invented sticky notes. This class had the reputation of being a "weeder" course, with a low pass rate. I knew this, yet my mindset remained the same: least amount of effort to get an A.

During the first semester, I became friends with another student with similar medical school ambitions. When I would go over to his apartment, he was always studying. I remember wondering, "Why is he studying so much?"

I shouldn't have been surprised when he got an A on the first exam, and I got a B.

With my fixed mindset, I did not view my B grade as a signal that I needed to work harder and study more. Instead, I chalked it up as "I wasn't familiar with how the professor wrote his exam questions."

As the first semester came to a close, I received a B–, the lowest grade I had ever received. My friend earned an A and posted one of the top grades in the class.

When interpreting this situation, my fixed mindset prevented me from seeing that my friend was gaining so much value from studying. Instead, it caused me to interpret the situation as he was naturally gifted at chemistry (a "have") and I was not (a "have-not"). This interpretation meant that for the next semester, rather than buckle down and study harder, I essentially gave up, not only on the class but also on my desire to become a medical doctor. I ended that semester with a C and in search of a new major. Ultimately, my fixed mindset limited how I thought about my situation, how much I learned, and how I behaved.

I wish I could say that my mindset only affected how I operated in this chemistry class, but truthfully, I carried it throughout my undergraduate education. While I never got a grade worse than a B since that class, my mindset prevented me from putting forth increased effort to learn and master the material in the classes that did not come naturally to me.

My experience is not unique. Carol Dweck has repeatedly found that because fixed mindset individuals want to look good and avoid challenge and effort, they naturally select courses of action that are easy and make them look good, ultimately limiting their learning, development, and future success. Specifically, when Dweck presents subjects with an option to redo an easy puzzle or try something harder, those with a fixed mindset tend to stick with the safe, easy puzzle to ensure success and recognition. Those with a growth mindset, on the other hand, question the value of such behavior and instead opt for the hard puzzle to push and develop themselves.

If your personal mindset assessment revealed more of a fixed mindset, consider the times when your fixed mindset prevented you from approaching challenges with optimism and from putting in enhanced effort. In those instances, were you more concerned with being a have or with developing yourself?

We do not need to think in terms of "haves" and "have-nots." That is a fixed mindset talking. A much more healthy and effective growth-minded perspective is "If it does not come naturally to me, it is only because I haven't put forth enough effort yet."

Summary

Remember Alan, the CEO of the nonprofit? While he operates within and navigates his role the best he can, his fixed mindset continually wreaks havoc on how he thinks, learns, and behaves.

This can be seen when Alan is presented with the option to move away from his outdated, tried-and-true leadership training program versus developing a new, cutting-edge program that involves new technology and learning processes to enhance the development of the leaders in his programs.

Not being aware of his fixed mindset and the non-conscious automatic programming that comes with it, Alan's fixed mindset prefers to stick with the tried-and-true program because he knows he won't fail and it won't require any additional effort. Further, as the cutting-edge program is just that—cutting-edge—it is going to require Alan to put forth effort to master more current leadership thought and to learn new technology and learning processes. Alan's fixed mindset doesn't like the idea of doing something new and putting forth significant effort. To him, doing something new means that there is a greater risk for failure. Further, putting forth effort to learn means that he has to admit that he is not currently a "have." Thus, Alan is quick to shut down any idea to update his programming.

Alan's fixed mindset makes him feel justified in his decision to stick with the tried-and-true option. But this same mindset simultaneously prevents him from seeing how this decision is limiting his personal growth and development and the value he can provide to his customers. Ultimately, it is a decision that is going to limit his success.

Chapter 7

THE POWER OF GROWTH MINDSETS TO DRIVE SUCCESS IN LIFE, WORK, AND LEADERSHIP

When we give ourselves permission to fail, we, at the same time, give ourselves permission to excel.

—Eloise Ristad

When it comes to success, who would you consider to be one of the most successful basketball players of all time? Surely, Michael Jordan is at the top or near the top of your list. He recited these lines in a Nike commercial:

I've missed more than 9,000 shots in my career. I've lost almost 300 games. Twenty-six times, I've been trusted to take the game-winning shot and missed. I've failed over and over and over again in my life. And that is why I succeed.

While this quote is related to his professional experience, he seems to carry this attitude in all aspects of his life. As a high school sophomore, he did not get the one roster spot on the varsity team reserved for a sophomore. While it was crushing, he used this failure to motivate himself. After receiving this news, he was in the gym every morning, long before the coaches arrived at school. Often, they had to run him out of the gym to get to class. Of this experience, Jordan said, "Whenever I was working out and got tired and figured I ought to stop, I'd close my eyes and see that list in the locker room without my name on it. That usually got me going again."

In his book *Principles*, Ray Dalio tells this story:

I once had a ski instructor who had also given lessons to Michael Jordan, the greatest basketball player of all time. Jordan, he told me, reveled in his mistakes, seeing each of them as an opportunity to improve. He understood that mistakes are like those little puzzles that, when you solve them, give you a gem. Every mistake that you make and learn from will save you from thousands of similar mistakes in the future.

Do these two accounts sound like Michael Jordan possessed a fixed mindset or a growth mindset? Surely, a growth mindset was a key foundational driver of his success.

During the more than 30 years of research on fixed and growth mindsets, much has been learned and discussed. However, if you boil it down to a singular comment, consider this statement that all mindset researchers seem to agree on: "Cultivating a growth mindset could be the single most important thing you ever do to help you achieve success." A growth mindset allows people to take on challenges and cope well with setbacks, both necessary ingredients for success— and both beyond the reach of those with a persistently fixed mindset.

In this chapter, we will explore how our fixed and growth mindsets drive our success in life, work, and leadership.

Success in Life

At a very basic level, who is going to live more successfully?

- Those who believe that they are stuck, unable to change, grow, and develop? Or those who believe that they can change, grow, and develop?

- Those who focus on being a "have" and looking good? Or those who focus on learning and growing to become better?
- Those who avoid challenges? Or those who embrace them?
- Those who see a momentary failure as a sign that they are a complete failure? Or those who see failure as a valuable step to improvement and success?
- Those who give up when the going gets tough? Or those who persist and push forward?

It seems pretty obvious that those with a growth mindset are mentally wired to see and operate in their world in ways that are much more conducive to success than those with a fixed mindset. We have seen this in the examples already discussed. Hopefully by diving into the life of Johnny Manziel, the life of Christopher Langan, the on-court antics of Draymond Green, my wife's development as a baker, my approach to my education, and Alan's approach to his work, you have seen how a fixed mindset causes us to put a cap on our effectiveness, success, and potential. Further, I hope by considering some all-time greats like Tom Brady, Steph Curry, and Michael Jordan, you have seen that what has led them to be so successful was less about their natural talents and abilities and much more about how they approached life. They are successful because they have the growth-mindset-fueled hallmarks of success: a love of learning, a tendency to seek challenges, valuing effort, and persisting in the face of obstacles.

For the most part, I have discussed success in terms of performance relative to one's potential or to others. While this is important, it is one facet of a successful life. Success in life goes way beyond performance. Other elements of a successful life include how happy we are with ourselves, the quality of our career, the quality of our relationships, and, if we are a parent, our effectiveness as a parent. Research on fixed and growth mindsets has some interesting takeaways associated with each of these facets of a successful life.

Based upon what has been covered thus far, who do you think is going to have higher levels of self-esteem, be happier with their lives, and be more confident: those with a growth mindset or those with a fixed mindset? I am sure you are thinking, a growth mindset. You are right! But why? When we have a fixed mindset, we are always comparing ourselves to others to determine whether we are a "have" or a "have-not." These consistent comparisons make us prone to see and be sensitive to the talents we don't have, the life we don't lead, and the ways we don't measure up. When we have a growth mindset, we are more prone to see the progress we have made, the blessings in our life, the opportunities on the horizon, and the value that we have.

Next, consider a recent research study published by Paul O'Keefe, Carol Dweck, and Greg Walton that has direct implications for our career and indirect implications for our relationships. Following the theme of this book, these researchers found that how we see our careers shapes how we operate within them. Specifically, they found that because those with a fixed mindset believe that their talents, abilities, and intelligence are fixed, they also believe that there is one right career that is a fit for them, and they will only be satisfied when they find their true passion. How does a fixed mindset individual determine whether or not they have found their fit and true passion? Primarily, it is through their assessment of how naturally and effortlessly their career comes to them. Those with a fixed mindset see the need for effort as a signal indicating that if they continue down that path, challenge and failure are possibilities, causing them to see the signal as a need to find another route. As long as one's career feels natural and effortless, they will continue to think that they have found their fit and true passion. But the instant difficulties arise and effort is required, those with a fixed mindset are quick to see such situations as evidence that they haven't yet found their fit and true passion, making them inclined to give up and leave their role instead of working through the difficulties and challenges.

On the other hand, the researchers found that growth-minded individuals see their careers very differently. Rather than believing that there is one right career or fit for them, they inherently believe that there are many options and opportunities available to them. Accordingly, they do not feel like they need to find their passion. Instead, they adhere more closely to the maxim "develop your passion." With this perspective, when challenges pop up and effort is required, they do not take it as a sign that they are on the wrong path; rather, they take it as a sign that they need to invest more and increase their efforts.

While the researchers didn't investigate this, I believe these same ideas translate to our relationships. Using the same rationale as above, I believe that when coming to select a partner or spouse, fixed mindset individuals tend to believe that they need to find their "true love" or "soul mate," the one who is the right fit for them. As long as the relationship feels natural and doesn't require too much effort, they will come to believe they have found their soul mate. But as soon as difficulties arise (as they inevitably will), they are prone to see these difficulties as a signal that they haven't found their soul mate and are much more inclined to leave the relationship.

Those with a growth mindset, on the other hand, are less inclined to believe there is one certain person who is right for them. They believe that a successful relationship is less about the right fit and more about sustained investment over time, and they recognize that every relationship will have its own challenges. When difficulties arise, they do not take it as a sign that they are incompatible and walk away; rather, they take it as a sign that they need to invest more and increase their efforts.

After reading this research, my main takeaway was that those with a fixed mindset seem to be programmed to take the path of least resistance when it comes to their careers and relationships, whereas those with a growth mindset are willing to take more challenging paths. The difference results in those with a fixed mindset ending up at the bottom with a poor view of the beauty around them, while those with a growth mindset end up at the top with the best vantage point of the beauty around them.

Finally, I want to share with you an interesting study related to parenting. I think all parents want the best for their children, and part of this means that they want their children to excel academically. Educational researchers Benjamin Matthes and Heidrun Stoeger found that parents' mindsets influence the mindsets of their children, how they work with their children related to their academics, and ultimately how well their children do academically. Comparing parents with a growth mindset to parents with a fixed mindset, they found that when parents have a growth mindset, their children are more likely to have a growth mindset, they are less likely to engage in controlling behavior to do homework or perform at a certain level, they are less likely to engage in homework-related conflict, and, perhaps unsurprisingly, their children are more likely to have higher academic performance.

As a parent myself, I find this completely fascinating. I want to be a parent who empowers my children to be their best, and I want to do so in a manner that builds trust and connection. After reading this study, I am inspired to develop more of a growth mindset so that I can create an even better environment for them to excel.

Based upon the accumulated research presented here, there is clear evidence that something as small as whether or not we believe people can change their talents, abilities, and intelligence undergirds our success across almost every important facet of our lives.

Do you believe that you and others can change? Do you care more about learning and growing than about looking good? Do you embrace rather than avoid challenges? Do you see failure as a valuable opportunity to improve and reach higher levels of success? Do you persist and push forward when the going gets tough?

If your answer is not a strong yes to each of those, can you see how you are not living up to your potential when it comes to your success across the most important facets of your life? Can you see how you are leaving opportunities on the table?

The beautiful thing about this is that living more fully in your potential and better seizing the opportunities in front of you does not require some sort of monumental effort. It only requires that you change how you see the world, swapping out your current lenses for new and improved models. We will discuss how you can do that more fully in the next chapter.

Success in Work

From about 2000 until 2013, Microsoft's market capitalization hovered at around $200 billion, and its stock price fluctuated around $26 per share. While a market capitalization of $200 billion is nothing to bat an eye at, Microsoft's stagnation meant that they were losing ground to their competitors. Near the turn of 2014, it is safe to say that Microsoft was not primed for future success.

Since 2014, Microsoft has been on a tear, and their market capitalization recently eclipsing $1 trillion, positioning it as one of the four most valuable companies in the world. It is on par with or exceeding Apple, Alphabet, and Amazon. Its stock price is now five times greater than it was during their stagnant period.

Does Microsoft seem much more primed for future success now? Certainly! What has been the difference?

Well, one thing is obvious: a new CEO. During the early part of 2014, Satya Nadella took the helm at Microsoft. He believes that the *C* in *CEO* stands for "curator of the organization's culture" and that it is the CEO's most important role. Changing Microsoft's culture has been his priority from day one. At the center of this focus has been a growth mindset.

Nadella joined Microsoft in 1992 and had seen both massive growth and long stagnation. After reading Carol Dweck's book *Mindset*, which focuses on fixed and growth mindsets, he realized that the root of Microsoft's stagnation was a fixed mindset culture. He described the culture as "Rigid. Each employee had to prove to everyone that he or she knew it all, and was the smartest person in the room. Accountability, delivering on time, and hitting the numbers trumped everything. Meetings were formal. Everything had to be planned in perfect detail before the meeting…Hierarchy and pecking order had taken control and spontaneity and creativity had suffered as a result." Further, he indicated that his leadership team was not adventurous, possessing "fear[s] of being ridiculed, of failing, of not looking like the smartest person in the room."

These are perfect descriptions of an organization that is prioritizing looking good over learning and growing. They are also perfect descriptions of an organization that is dying. There is no life, creativity, or innovation in rigidity, formality, and fear.

Consider Pixar Animation. It is among the most creative and innovative companies on the planet. From 1995 to 2019, Pixar has released 20 films. Of those, 15 are in the top 50 for highest-grossing animated films ever. Seven peaked in the top five at the box office. And that doesn't include the box office hits that Disney Animation released after the Pixar/Disney merger: *Frozen*, *Zootopia*, *Moana*, and *Tangled*.

At the center of this creativity and massive success is Ed Catmull, the co-founder and president of Pixar Animation and also president of Disney Animation. The way he sees it, his job is to "create a fertile environment, keep it healthy, and watch for the things that undermine it…[including] the blocks that get in the way, often without us noticing, and hinder the creativity that resides within any thriving company."

From his experience, he has learned that what most hinders creativity is the fixed mindset fear of failure that is consistently trying to creep in. He recognizes that for most everyone, the message "failure is bad" has been drilled into our heads, largely because we tend to believe that failure is a signal that one is not smart. When we fail, it is accompanied with strong and visceral emotional reactions, including shame and embarrassment. This pain and our desire to avoid it blinds us to our understanding of its worth.

Knowing this, Catmull is focused on intentionally maintaining a growth-minded culture as the antidote to this fixed mindset fear of failure. He helps Pixar employees understand and get past the short-term negative emotions that come with failure and see that failure has very important long-term positive effects. Rather than vilifying failure, he encourages it.

Why encourage failure? Catmull states, "Failure is an inevitable consequence of doing something new. And, as such, should be seen as valuable. Without [it], we'd have no originality." He goes on to say, "Failure is a manifestation of learning and exploration. If you aren't experiencing failure, then you are making a far worse mistake: You are being driven by the desire to avoid it. And, this strategy—trying to avoid failure by outthinking it—dooms you to fail."

If employees operate in a fear-based, failure-adverse culture, they will avoid risk and be hesitant to explore new areas and ideas. They will resort to the safe, accepted route. Their work will not be innovative, nor will it have an impact. Pixar understands that if they want their employees to break new ground, do truly creative and innovative work, take big strides rather than small insignificant steps, and truly make an impact, they must create a culture that is not just open to failure, but values it.

Evidence of this culture and its power comes from Andrew Stanton, writer and/or director for *A Bug's Life, Finding Nemo, Finding Dory,* and all of the *Toy*

Story films. Stanton's growth mindset has fueled his personal philosophies toward failure. He is known for telling his team to "Fail early and fail fast," and "Be wrong as fast as you can." Further, he believes that if someone is trying something new, creative, or innovative at work, we should not look at it any differently than learning to ride a bike or play guitar. We should never expect someone to learn something new without toppling over or playing the wrong notes. Further, when someone does topple, we never take their bike or guitar away. With these philosophies, he created a culture among his team where they felt safe to explore, tackle big problems, and be individually creative and empowered.

This attitude and willingness to fail and adjust is agility, and it not only has organizational and team implications, but also personal implications.

Consider Pete Docter, the director of *Monsters, Inc.* When Docter started this project, no one other than John Lasseter had directed a Pixar film. The stakes were high and Docter was under a microscope.

We know *Monsters, Inc.* as a story of three characters that we have come to love: Sully, the big blue monster; Mike, the one-eyed green monster; and Boo, a fearless, preverbal toddler. When the idea for the movie was first pitched, however, it was about a 30-year-old man coping with a cast of frightening characters that only he could see—a much different movie.

How did *Monsters, Inc.* go from the original idea to something very different? In short: failure. Docter and his team made countless wrong turns over the course of several years before the movie found its true north. Each of those wrong turns heightened the pressure he and his team were under. However, Docter kept the attitude that they wouldn't know how to most strongly manifest the core idea of the movie—monsters are real, and they scare kids for a living—without experimenting, testing, and reevaluating. Docter recognized that when you are breaking new ground, the process of discovery prevails. He never believed that a failed approach meant that they should give up. Rather, he saw each idea leading them closer to the best option. Catmull states, "When experimentation is seen as necessary and productive, not a frustrating waste of time, people will enjoy their work—even when it is confounding them."

Because of Docter's growth mindset, he was not stuck on his original idea. He believed that he and it could grow into something greater, something that would better capture and convey his core message. Because of his agility, *Monsters, Inc.* has become the household hit we love today.

From decades at the helm of Pixar and later Disney Animation, Catmull summarizes the mindset we should take toward failure:

While [failure] is scary to many, I would argue that we should be far more terrified of the opposite approach. Being too risk-averse causes many companies to stop innovating and to reject new ideas, which is the first step on the path to irrelevance. Probably more companies hit the skids for this reason than because they dared to push boundaries and take risks—and, yes, to fail. To be a truly creative company, you must start things that might fail.

This is where Microsoft was when Nadella took over: the path to irrelevance. Nadella recognized it and needed to do something about it.

To help make the shift from being fixed minded to being growth minded, Nadella declared that the company would focus on becoming "learn-it-alls" rather than know-it-alls. He developed and promoted a new growth-minded mission statement: "Empower every person and every organization on the planet to achieve more." What a great mission statement! It gets leaders and employees to be forward thinking, causing them to naturally ask the question: "How do I grow to help others to grow?"

Clearly, this renewed focus has paid huge dividends, both literally and figuratively.

Success in Leadership

Have you ever heard of CEO disease? This malady occurs when someone works his or her way up the corporate ladder and progressively becomes less self-aware. They increasingly believe in their omnipotence, surround themselves with yes-people, and respond brutally to opposition.

How prevalent is CEO disease among leaders and managers? The reality is that poor and dysfunctional leaders are much more common than we would like to admit. Two statistics suggest this:

- 40% of Americans rank their boss as "bad."
- 75% of employees report their boss is the worst and most stressful part of their job.

While these statistics likely make our stomach churn, what fascinates me is that when I am training and working with leaders, they all say the same thing: they are trying the best they can. I believe it. This has led me to wonder how so many leaders can be trying the best they can, yet collectively be so ineffective, or even destructive.

The answer is rooted in their mindsets. Leaders' negative mindsets drive them to think and act in ways that seem logical but are actually destructive, leading to the negative statistics above.

Let's return to Alan from Chapter 1. If you recall, Alan had a turnover problem in his organization. Those who left, or in some instances were forced to leave, were those who fought back against Alan's dysfunctional leadership. In other words, they were not yes-people. To observers, it was obvious that he wanted to be the star of the show and felt threatened by employees who came up with ideas to improve upon Alan's prior choices or pushed back against his subpar decisions. But Alan's fixed mindset did not allow him to see this. Instead, he justified his actions as "rooting out the weeds" and "creating a cohesive team." He spun his actions in a positive way that made him feel good about himself. But the effect was that he limited the effectiveness of the organization, enhanced turnover costs, and created a negative and fearful culture. His fixed mindset blinded him to how dysfunctional he really was.

While each negative mindset covered in this book has similar blinding and self-justifying effects, fixed mindsets may be a dominant and common cause of poor and dysfunctional leadership, particularly at the top. This is evidenced by surveys I conducted with two large organizations. The first was with the top 130 executives of a Fortune 10 organization. The survey revealed that 42% of their leaders had a fixed mindset—20 percentage points higher than the next most common negative mindset. The second was with 263 top executives of one of the largest telecom companies in Europe. In this case, 55% of their leaders had a fixed mindset—10 percentage points higher than the next most common negative mindset.

This should lead you to wonder:

- Why is a fixed mindset so common among leaders?
- Why is having a fixed mindset so destructive for leaders?
- Why is it so valuable to have growth-minded leaders?

Why is a fixed mindset so common among leaders? Remember, a primary concern of those with a fixed mindset is that they need to protect their image, since they do not believe they can change their talents, abilities, and intelligence. Leaders recognize that most organizations and social structures expect leaders to appear positive. Thus, when put into a leadership position, most leaders naturally feel social and cultural pressure to consistently appear at their best, even infallible. To keep their ideal image up, they desire to always be in control of the conditions they operate under.

If leaders are not conscious of this, this pressure and need for control does two things. First, it causes them to develop a fixed mindset, the onset of CEO disease. Second, if one already has a fixed mindset, it amplifies the negative aspects of that mindset, causing CEO disease to really take root.

Why is having a fixed mindset so destructive for leaders? For the answer to this question, we turn to what management scholars refer to as upper-echelon theory. Its basic premise is that what an organization's highest-level leaders focus on and pay attention to influences the information they process, the decisions they make, and ultimately the direction and success of the organization. What dictates what leaders pay attention to and how they process information? No surprise here: their mindsets. This theory implies that the mindsets of only a few people in high-level leadership positions have a disproportionate effect on organizational success, and the organization's level of success is contingent upon what its top-level leaders' mindsets are programmed to focus on: looking good or learning and growing.

Thus, when an organization's leaders possess a fixed mindset, they generally have a disproportionately negative effect on their organizations. Since their overwhelming desire is to look good and be seen as a "have," their natural, primary, and consistent focus and priority becomes the validation of their superiority and greatness. This focus undergirds everything they do, overriding their desires to actually make a positive impact on the organization.

Their fixed mindset causes them to self-protect as opposed to organizationally advance.

Let me give you an example of a fixed mindset leader and how it played out for him: Lee Iacocca. Iacocca was the president, CEO, and chairman of Chrysler from 1979 to 1992. He was known for his large ego, initially hailed as a conquering hero after he revitalized Chrysler's image and revived the company from its deathbed (although historical hindsight has shown that Chrysler was really saved by a government bailout and some well-timed interventions against Japanese imports).

Business commentators have suggested that Iacocca, along with his ego, star power, and his best-selling autobiography in which he called himself a hero, changed the leadership landscape across American businesses—and not for the positive. Until Iacocca, the general image of the American CEO had been of a buttoned-down organization man who was essentially bland and characterless. But with Iacocca's fame and perceived success, CEOs became America's superheroes, obtaining celebrity status. Of this, Jim Collins, the author of *Good to Great* and *Built to Last*, stated: "In the 1980s, there was a sea change in the way the media and the culture at large responded to CEOs. And you can pinpoint that change to one single event: the publication of the Iacocca book. That was the moment when it became clear that everything was different." Thus, the myth of the CEO as a superhero was born. Companies everywhere wanted their own Iacocca.

These same commentators suggest that if not for Iacocca, people like Donald Trump, Steve Jobs, and Elon Musk would not have been put on the pedestals that they so gladly seized. In fact, James Surowiecki of *Slate* goes so far to suggest that "if it weren't for Iacocca, it is unlikely that we would be talking about Enron and WorldCom today."

If you look at the cover of Iacocca's autobiography, you get a sense of Iacocca's fixed-mindset-fueled drive. He is leaning back in his office chair in shirt and tie, and his hands are behind his head in an extreme power pose. It seems clear that Iacocca wanted to be seen as the top dog.

Throughout his leadership, he demonstrated a consistent drive to prove himself as a "have," to prove his greatness. He was more focused on advancing himself than Chrysler. This was evidenced in a variety of ways. From the inside, Chrysler insiders joked that Iacocca stood for "I Am Chairman of Chrysler Corporation Always." From the outside, it was clear that he spent too much company time and resources on things that would enhance his public image—all in an effort to increase Chrysler's stock—and not enough time on what would make the company profitable in the long run. For example, he kept employee pay low and limited investment in manufacturing improvement, while simultaneously investing $2 million on renovating his corporate suite at the Waldorf in New York.

Additional evidence of Iacocca's fixed mindset wreaking havoc came when Chrysler started to struggle again after its initial revitalization. With shareholders displeased with Chrysler's performance, Iacocca passed the blame and made excuses, rather than taking ownership and investigating the true root of the problem. When Japanese auto manufacturers (e.g., Toyota, Honda) started taking over the American market, rather than seeking to improve Chrysler's cars, Iacocca worked with the Reagan administration to impose tariffs and quotas that would stop Japanese manufacturers. *The New York Times* chided, "The solution lies in making better cars in this country, not in angrier excuses about Japan."

Commenting on Iacocca's tenure as CEO of Chrysler, Jim Collins clearly articulates Iacocca's fixed-mindset-fueled desire to self-protect as opposed to organizationally advance:

> Lee Iacocca…saved Chrysler from the brink of catastrophe, performing one of the most celebrated (and deservedly so) turnarounds in American business history. Chrysler rose to a height of 2.9 times the market at a point about halfway through his tenure. Then, however, he diverted his attention to making himself one of the most celebrated CEOs in American business history…[He] appeared regularly on talk shows like the *Today* show and *Larry King Live*, personally starred in over eighty commercials, entertained the idea of running for president of the United States (quoted at one point, "Running Chrysler has been a bigger job than running the country…I could handle the national economy in six

months."), and widely promoted his autobiography (sold seven million copies)…Iacocca's personal stock soared, but in the second half of his tenure, Chrysler's stock fell 31 percent behind the general market.

This fixed mindset effect is not unique to Iacocca. One way researchers have tried to measure CEO's focus on appearance and being seen as a "have" is by looking at (1) how much they are compensated above and beyond the next highest paid executive and (2) the size of the CEO's photograph in their company's annual report, a decision the CEO usually makes. In these studies, researchers found that the larger the relative pay and size of the CEO's photograph in the annual report, the more overconfident the CEOs are in their projections and the more likely they are to engage in fraud.

Carol Dweck sums up the negative impact of fixed mindset leaders by stating that the standard operating procedure for fixed mindset leaders is to "blame others, cover mistakes, pump up the stock prices, crush rivals and critics, and screw the little guy." And what make the situation worse is that because of their fixed mindset, such leaders see these standard operating procedures as being best practices.

Why is it so valuable to have growth-minded leaders? A growth mindset allows leaders to value and focus on advancing their organization above and beyond their own self-image. There are four main ways growth mindset leaders operate differently than fixed mindset leaders, which makes a world of difference for their organizations and the people they lead and manage.

First, rather than focus on appearance and proving themselves, those with a growth mindset focus on doing what is necessary for success, even if it doesn't make them look good. This allows them to make decisions that profit the company in the long run.

A great example is Anne Mulcahy, the chairperson and CEO of Xerox Corporation from 2001 to 2009. Under her leadership, considered legendary in the corporate world, she helped Xerox survive through financial disasters that brought the company to the brink of bankruptcy, and made Xerox profitable in a few short years. *Fortune* named her "the hottest turnaround act since Lou Gerstner."

When Mulcahy first become CEO of Xerox, rather than posturing and doing what was best for her or what made her look good, she did the necessary things to ensure the organization was successful, even if it didn't necessarily send the most positive image. For example, in order to better understand the company and how her decisions affected the organizations' bottom line, she would take large binders home over the weekends and absorb them as if she had a final exam on Monday morning. She even had someone teach her Balance Sheet 101. These types of behaviors do not necessarily send the signal that she was the most capable and qualified to operate as CEO, but she showed she cared more about advancing the organization than protecting herself and her image. It makes me wonder how many fixed mindset leaders would allow themselves to learn Balance Sheet 101.

Second, rather than pass blame or make excuses (self-protection behaviors), those with a growth mindset are able to take ownership and responsibility, allowing for positive change to occur. Taking ownership and responsibility for mistakes or errors does not necessarily make a leader look good in the moment, but without it, the organization is doomed to squander opportunities.

Since we just identified Mulcahy as being "the hottest turnaround act since Lou Gerstner," let's dive into what made him so successful. Gerstner was the chairman and CEO of IBM from April 1993 until 2002. During his tenure, he took a company that, in 1993, posted the biggest loss in the history of corporate America ($8 billion) and guided it through a massive organizational change that led to a market capitalization rise from $29 billion to $168 billion during his nine-year tenure. That's astonishing. Even then, a massive organizational change might be an understatement, as IBM completely changed its business model, moving away from primarily focusing on computer mainframes to integrated information technology solutions.

Unlike Iacocca, Gerstner didn't blame external market conditions for IBM's lack of success. Nor did he continually try to gain publicity. By not doing these things, he was able to tackle the root causes associated with IBM's decline. With IBM losing badly to Microsoft, HP, and Apple in the computer turf wars, Gerstner quickly focused on internal factors that were driving a lack of productivity (likely created by leaders with a fixed mindset): prestige and entitlement. He flattened the organization, disbanded the management committee (the ultimate power role for IBM executives), opened up to advice from external partners, and fired those who liked to play politics and indulge in internal intrigue. He created a growth-minded culture that collectively focused on learning, development, and advancement, which resulted in the sixfold rise in market capitalization.

Third, rather than get defensive around people who challenge them, those with a growth mindset seek out those people. Growth mindset leaders are frequently found saying, "I try to hire people smarter than myself," even if it means pushback or criticism. In taking this approach, growth mindset leaders recognize that they have weaknesses. Rather than hide those weaknesses like a fixed mindset leader, they bring in people to overcome them, allowing for a healthier balance of strengths, skill set, and power.

An example of such a leader is Ed Catmull. Even before his Pixar career, Catmull realized that if he wanted his groups and teams to be successful and meet the challenges associated with pushing the boundaries of technology, he needed to hire people smarter and more highly qualified than himself. In fact, in his first opportunity to lead an organization and assemble a team, one of the first people he interviewed was an already established leader with a sparkling resume: Alvy Ray Smith. Of this situation, Catmull admits, "I had conflicting feelings when I met Alvy because, frankly, he seemed more qualified to lead the lab than I was. I can still remember the uneasiness in my gut, that instinctual twinge spurred by a potential threat: This, I thought, could be the guy who takes my job one day. I hired him anyway." Catmull's growth mindset allowed him the ability to advance the organization rather than protect himself. He knew that to ensure his lab succeeded, he needed to attract the sharpest minds, which meant leaving behind his insecurities.

Consider what Catmull learned from this situation early in his career. It is something that is possible only with a growth mindset:

> Ever since, I've made a policy of trying to hire people who are smarter than I am. The obvious payoffs of exceptional people are that they innovate, excel, and generally make your company—and,

by extension, you—look good. But there is another, less obvious, payoff that only occurred to me in retrospect. The act of hiring Alvy changed me as a manager: By ignoring my fear, I learned that the fear was groundless. Over the years, I have met people who took what seemed the safer path and were the lesser for it. By hiring Alvy, I had taken a risk, and that risk yielded the highest reward—a brilliant, committed teammate. I had wondered in graduate school how I could ever replicate the singular environment of [my graduate program]. Now, suddenly, I saw the way. Always take a chance on better, even if it seems threatening.

Fourth, rather than being focused solely on their own advancement, leaders with a growth mindset develop those they lead. This is because when a fixed mindset leader sees employees as being unable to improve their talents, abilities, and intelligence, he or she sees little reason to invest time, effort, and resources in helping them improve. Thus, it is only those with a growth mindset that allow themselves to devote time, effort, and resources to helping them.

In fact, in a unique research study, Peter Heslin, Don VandeWalle, and Gary Latham found that managers with a growth mindset give both higher quantity and higher quality feedback. Further, they found that managers with a growth mindset were much more willing to coach a poor-performing employee, implying that fixed mindset managers are more likely to give up on them. In other words, when a fixed mindset leader does not feel another is performing up to expectations, the leader will seek to let the person go as opposed to identifying why the person is underperforming (e.g., does not have the materials or resources needed), and will fail to see or address the reason for underperformance.

Because growth mindset leaders are primarily focused on learning and growing, as opposed to looking good and validating themselves, they do not have egos to protect. They feel no need to prove and display their superiority. This allows them to devote their time and resources on the needs and success of those they lead.

Summary

Isn't it amazing to see how something as small as the lenses one uses to view their world plays such a significant role in their success across their life, work, and leadership?

Now, let's go to work on creating and developing a strong growth mindset.

Chapter 8

DEVELOPING A GROWTH MINDSET

The problem human beings face is not that we aim too high and fail, but that we aim too low and succeed.

—Unknown

E arlier, I focused on Johnny Manziel and how his fixed mindset drove him to thinking, learning, and behaving in ways that did not allow him to take advantage of his natural talent. In the 1980s, another athlete struggled in a similar way because of his fixed mindset. But, later in life, he was able to develop a growth mindset, which allowed him to literally change the game of baseball by ushering in the use of statistical analyses and projections to more accurately assess the value of baseball players, something all teams now utilize. This athlete and now executive vice president of baseball operations for the Oakland Athletics is Billy Beane. The best-selling book and box office smash movie *Moneyball* are about him.

While attending Mt. Carmel High School near San Diego, Beane continually captivated professional scouts and teams. He was a natural, a true five-tool player: someone who excels at hitting for average, hitting for power, running the bases, throwing, and fielding. He was one of the greatest high school baseball players ever to come from Southern California, which is saying a lot.

Beane was an all-around athletic phenom. In addition to excelling on the baseball diamond, he was a star basketball and football player. He was also a 4.0 student, then a perfect GPA. Stanford offered him a dual scholarship to play baseball and football (as a quarterback, the heir apparent to John Elway, who was on his way to NFL stardom). He was a top prospect in the 1980 Major League Baseball draft. The New York Mets considered taking him with the first overall selection, but because teams believed he would attend Stanford rather than sign professionally, the Mets selected him 23rd overall.

Unfortunately, despite his over-the-top talent, Beane possessed a fixed mindset, affecting his ability to persevere through failure. In baseball, failure is a major part of the game. The average on-base percentage is about .320, meaning a batter will reach base only 32% of the time. In the book *Moneyball*, Michael Lewis writes, "It wasn't merely that [Beane] didn't like to fail; it was if he didn't know how to fail." Beane saw each out, whether a hard-hit line drive out or strikeout, as an indication that he was a failure. Seeing himself as someone with fixed talent, he was left to internalize this failure, eroding his self-confidence.

Unfortunately, Beane's fixed mindset never allowed him to reach his playing potential. Much of his career was spent in the minor leagues, bounced from the Mets to the Minnesota Twins, Detroit Tigers, and Oakland Athletics farm systems. Weary of the lifestyle, he asked for and received a job as a scout for the Oakland A's in 1990. Three years later, he was promoted to assistant general manager. In 1997, he became the A's general manager.

During Beane's stint as assistant general manager, the ownership of the A's changed. With this change in 1995, the amount of money the A's spent on players dove from being among the highest in the Major Leagues to among the lowest. This made Beane's job of putting together a winning baseball team difficult, as he did not have a budget to hire the most talented players.

This is when Beane's mindset began to change. Because he was unable to win with the A's payroll limitations, Beane developed a player selection system that emphasized on-field productivity over the dominant paradigm within baseball: perceived talent. As Carol Dweck put it, "They didn't buy talent, they bought mindset."

Beane's growth-mindset-fueled experiment came to fruition in 2002. The A's won 103 games that year—including, at one point, 20 wins in a row—and the division championship, despite having the second lowest payroll in baseball.

Needless to say, this success made a splash. Ever since, MLB teams have used statistical analytics to make decisions around acquiring players and how to play them during games (e.g., where to place them in the batting order, where they should position themselves in the field), truly changing the way baseball is managed and played.

Changing Your Mindset Is Possible

Everyone can change their mindsets to bring about greater success. Researchers Joshua Aronson, Carrie Fried, and Catherine Good found that by just having students write about working hard in spite of their difficulties (a task to develop a growth mindset), their engagement and performance in school increases relative to students in a control condition. Over and over again, researchers have found that small exercises like this can have significant effects on attitude and behavior for up to six weeks.

To fully grasp how to change our mindsets, it is helpful to go back to the cognitive science associated with mindsets. Recall that our mindsets are neural connections in our prefrontal cortex that are stronger and fire more rapidly than other neural connections. These fast-firing neural connections cause us to quickly process information in predictable and repeated ways over time.

This implies that when we talk about changing our mindsets, we are really talking about rewiring our brain or, more specifically, the neural connections in our brain. We must reduce the strength of our negative mindset neural connections and strengthen our positive mindset neural connections.

To do this, we will do well to remember this adage: neurons that fire together wire together. Essentially all we need to do is exercise our positive mindset neural connections.

This process of rewiring our brain is not unlike becoming fluent at counting to 10 in a foreign language. This initially involves concerted effort to learn the words associated with each of the numbers. From there, we need to engage in relatively small, yet intentional, daily actions to practice counting in the new language. Over the course of a few weeks, we will gradually get to the point where counting to 10 in this new language comes naturally to us. Voilà, we have rewired our brain.

One challenge those with a fixed mindset face when changing and improving their mindsets is that their current mindset is tuned into the idea that people can't change their current wiring. Based upon her personal experience of moving from a fixed to a growth mindset, Carol Dweck wrote, "I realized why I'd always been so concerned about mistakes and failures. And, I recognized for the first time that I had a choice." Rewiring our brain and changing from a fixed mindset involves making a choice: believing that we can change.

One suggestion for developing this belief is to learn about just how malleable and plastic your brain really is. One great source for learning about brain plasticity is through TED and TEDx talks. If you do a YouTube search for "TED and brain plasticity," you will get over a dozen hits for some really great talks. Also, let me recommend a book called *The Brain That Changes Itself: Stories of Personal Triumph from the Frontiers of Brain Science*, by Norman Doidge. A description of the book reads:

An astonishing new science called neuroplasticity is overthrowing the centuries-old notion that the human brain is immutable…We see a woman born with half a brain that rewired itself to work as a whole, blind people who learn to see, learning disorders cured, IQs raised, aging brains rejuvenated, stroke patients learning to speak, children with cerebral palsy learning to move with more grace, depression and anxiety disorders successfully treated, and lifelong character traits changed. Using these marvelous stories to probe mysteries of the body, emotion, love, sex, culture, and education, Dr. Doidge has written an immensely moving, inspiring book that will permanently alter the way we look at our brains, human nature, and human potential.

Once we believe that we can change our mindsets, then we will have the motivation to learn the language of mindsets.

Step 1: Learn about Fixed and Growth Mindsets and Identify Their Cues

Until reading this section, you may have not known anything about fixed or growth mindsets. Without these labels and a basic understanding of what they are, you are powerless to introspect about and improve your mindsets.

But once you have labels and a basic understanding, you can objectify them. They become something that you can assess, focus on, and adjust. Putting labels on and learning about specific mindsets is perhaps the most empowering part of the process. And you are well on your way by now.

With this basic understanding, you are prepared to identify the cues associated with each mindset. Knowing such cues enhances your ability to more fully awaken to the role the your fixed or growth mindset is playing in your life.

Signals of a fixed mindset include:

- Feeling the need to prove your intelligence, talent, or superiority.
- Valuing status, hierarchies, and being in control.
- Feeling like you do not want to do something solely because it seems difficult.
- Focusing more on identifying and hiring top talent than developing current employees.
- Giving excuses and blame when things go wrong, as opposed to taking ownership.
- Looking for opportunities to gain power.
- Seeing others as either "haves" or "have-nots."
- Feeling a need to be superior to others.
- Wanting to hire yes-people over people who will push you with new and different perspectives.

- Seeing self-help books or other learning opportunities as things that make you feel bad or guilty.
- Quickly losing interest in a task if it does not come naturally to you
- Feeling like you want "out" after not doing as well as you would like.
- Feeling threatened by the success of others.
- Getting defensive easily when you receive constructive criticism.
- Sticking with what is familiar when faced with a choice between doing something that you are familiar with versus something that will push you to learn.

Signals of a growth mindset include:

- Getting excited about challenges and the opportunities they allow for learning and growth.
- Seeking to break down status barriers and hierarchies.
- Focusing more on developing talent as opposed to hiring top talent.
- Taking ownership when things go wrong.
- Looking for opportunities to share your power.
- Believing that everyone has an equal opportunity to succeed, and if they aren't succeeding, wondering what resources they lack (as opposed to what talents they lack).
- Wanting to work with and hire people you can learn from and who complement your areas of weakness.
- Seeing self-help books or other learning opportunities as things that excite and energize you.
- Being willing to dig in and try harder if something does not come naturally to you.
- Feeling energized by the success of others.
- Being willing to digest and explore constructive criticism.
- Choosing the challenging task when faced with a choice between doing something that you are familiar with and something that will push you to learn.

Step 2: Become Aware of Your Current Mindsets

With a knowledge of the different mindsets and their cues, you become able to assess and awaken to your current mindset. This may be easier said than done if you are entrenched in a fixed mindset.

Let me share a conversation I recently had with a college president. Early one morning, I received an email invitation to guide a leadership development session for a college's cabinet, which included the president and eight vice presidents. The initial email indicated they wanted to engage in some form of a self-assessment. I assumed that they were aware of my mindset assessment and were interested in taking it. I asked for more information and attached some information about my mindset assessment.

A couple of hours later, the president gave me a call. She informed me that she wanted me to do a team-building exercise and was quick to say that she didn't think they needed to talk about mindsets because they "knew all about fixed and growth mindsets." Then, she sent a signal indicating that she probably didn't know as much about these mindsets as she thought she did, because she spoke about how each has their pros and cons.

I asked her what she considered to be the purpose of doing a team-building exercise.

She told me that the college was going through a really bumpy time, and then listed a number of issues that they were facing, including:

- A variety of external factors leading to reduced student applications for enrollment.
- Three new members of the cabinet causing discomfort among the divisions that roll up to them.
- A number of recent whistle-blower complaints.
- The faculty have banded together to formally complain about the administration.

Because of these issues, she and the cabinet felt like they were fighting fires all over the college. She wanted a session to help them build resilience as a group and that would be a positive experience among all the chaos.

I asked her, "How does your team get along? Do they work well together?"

"Yes," she replied. "It is the best cabinet I've had in my 13-year tenure."

A little perplexed by this, I summarized by saying, "Your college is facing a number of problems that seem to be mindset-related, and rather than address these problems, you want a team-building session for a team that you feel works together well?"

It was clear that we were not a good fit, so we moved to end the call. I don't think she liked me implying that she and her cabinet could use some leadership and mindset development, so just before hanging up, she decided to give me a sucker punch and said, "My assistant told me to tell you that your proposed price was unreasonable." I had to chuckle because I listed a price that was almost half my typical rate, and they are one of the most expensive colleges to attend in the country.

While the college president said she "knew" about fixed and growth mindsets, she was not aware of her fixed mindset, which led her to run from and avoid problems, and prevented her from being willing to receive feedback, either from those in the college or myself. I was left wondering if she felt her cabinet was the best in her tenure because they were all yes-people who kept her on her pedestal, unwilling to push back against her dominating leadership.

Without an accurate understanding of our current mindsets and their implications, we will have little motivation to enhance our mindsets.

There are three ways that you can take the next step beyond understanding the difference between fixed and growth mindsets and more fully awaken to your current mindsets.

First, reflect inward. Introspect to determine the degree to which you value looking good and feel the need to validate yourself and your talents, abilities, and intelligence. Also, use the cues listed above, and seek to identify examples of when you have seen those cues in your life.

Second, take the personal mindset assessment linked to earlier in the book if you haven't done so already. This will help you identify the degree to which you possess a fixed or growth mindset relative to thousands of others.

Third, reach outward. This is probably the most difficult step but can be the most beneficial for identifying your current mindset. Take the opportunity to ask those closest to you, workers and friends alike, whether they think you have a fixed or growth mindset, how they have seen your mindset in action, and how it has affected them.

Step 3: Identify Your Destination and Chart Your Course

Once you have a grasp on your current mindset—your starting point—identify the mindset that you want to possess. This is your destination. Knowing both your starting point and destination empowers you to chart a course for mindset improvement.

This is where the rubber meets the road and you engage in specific efforts to shift your neural connections to rely more heavily upon your growth mindset connections. Just as learning to fluently count to 10 in a different language takes intentional and repeated practice, so does shifting our mindsets.

At first, this won't come naturally. When we are faced with a challenge, we are going to be cognitively inclined to jump in line with our fixed mindset neural connections quickly firing. Instead, we have to slow down, become more conscious, and, rather than react, choose to thoughtfully respond.

Research has found that one of the best ways to improve our ability to do this is to meditate. A couple of years ago, I had never meditated and saw it as some hippy-dippy practice. But as I got into the neuroscience behind mindsets, I was presented with more and more research lauding the praises of meditation. In fact, research has found that meditation leads to all of the following benefits, among many others:

- Reduces mind wandering
- Helps with directing attention amid competing demands
- Reduces attentional resources to process distractions
- Improves one's abilities to process and respond to novel information
- Improves one's creativity, divergent and convergent thinking, and problem solving
- Helps one not react strongly to negative stressors and better cope with stress

- Helps one respond more positively to goal or constructive feedback
- Shortens the time it takes for negative emotions to dissipate
- Helps create a healthy psychological distance from one's work
- Helps one better process information and behave more rationally
- Helps one carry more positive emotional tones
- Helps one develop more effective relationships with others
- Helps one have higher communication quality (listening, increased awareness, and less evaluative judgments)
- Helps one have greater empathy, compassion, and respect
- Helps one more effectively deal with and resolve conflict
- Helps one read the environment more accurately and less subject to the potential distortions of internal biases
- Helps one create a more psychologically safe environment
- Helps one be more satisfied with their job
- Helps one be more authentic and optimistic
- Helps one be more resilient when facing adversity, conflict, or failure
- Helps one be more comfortable with change
- Helps one be more intentional about their work
- Helps one have more autonomous motivation (driven to pursue activities perceived as being important, valued, and/or enjoyable)
- Helps one have higher job performance
- Helps one engage in more ethical behaviors, more prosocial behaviors, and less deviant behaviors

Essentially meditation is the practice of setting aside time devoted to attempting to become fully present and aware. It generally involves focusing on your breathing as a way to let your mind be fully present. While this is an important aspect of meditation, the most critical aspect occurs as your mind wanders, as it inevitably will. When this occurs, it is important that you become conscious of the fact that it has wandered and come back to focus on your breathing. It is this practice of yo-yoing in and out of present consciousness that strengthens our brain's ability to consciously override our natural inclination to react to our quick-to-fire negative mindset neural connection, and instead consciously respond and rely upon our slower-to-fire positive mindset neural connection.

As whole, meditation doesn't necessarily shift our mindsets, but it does enhance our capability to do so.

Let me give you some specific recommendations to shift your mindset from being more fixed to being more growth. Since shifting mindsets requires consistent and repeated practice over time, I recommend alternating across these ideas on a day-to-day basis. Over the course of a month or so, you will be well on your way to becoming fluent with your new positive mindset.

- Journal. Write about a time you double failed—that is, write about a time you failed at something, and then you failed again because you chose to not learn from it. Write about a time you singled failed, where you failed and chose to learn from it. Write about times in your life where you have taken on a challenge and succeeded. Show yourself that you have done it before and you can do it again.
- Read and learn more about fixed and growth mindsets. Read Carol Dweck's book *Mindset*. I also recommend reading *You Are a Badass* by Jen Sincero. Look up articles online on the topic. Search my blog at https://www.ryangottfredson.com/blog.
- Watch videos that promote the mindset that you want to develop. Eduardo Briceno has two great TEDx talks on the topic, as does Amy Purdy (see her talk "Living beyond Limits"). Watch movies that show people rising up and conquering a challenge despite all odds like *Rocky*, *Rudy*, *Remember the Titans*, *October Sky*, and *Hidden Figures*. Nick Vujicic, a man born with no arms or legs, is a public speaker with some great motivational speeches that can be found on YouTube.
- Have small group discussions about fixed and growth mindsets. Where have you seen them recently in your life or in the lives of those you live or work with? What have the results been? In this process, try your best to teach others what you know about each mindset. I find that I learn the best by teaching.

Step 4: Let Go of Your Prevailing Mindsets

Changing our mindsets by engaging in the three steps presented above is not hard, but it does take concerted effort. It is this concerted effort part that we often make difficult, for two reasons. First, it involves adopting new habits. Second, for some, it can be scary.

It is scary because we have become accustomed to seeing the world in a particular way. We likely identify with how we currently see the world and see this perspective as an important part of ourselves. Thus, for some, the idea of changing one's mindset will make them feel like a sellout.

Think of the stereotypical "my way or the highway" manager, like Alan in Chapter 1 or Lee Iacocca. Their leadership style was driven by their need to look good. This self-justifiable, egocentric perspective became a part of who they considered themselves to be. If they were to change, they might think that they were betraying themselves, feeling soft, or admitting defeat. The reality is different: they would not be betraying themselves but improving themselves.

Admittedly, seeing the world in a new and different way can be an uncertain, or even scary, proposition. Consider an adult who has never drunk alcohol now facing a proposition to drink. That person is likely fearful to let go of their stance toward alcohol because they are uncertain about how drinking will affect them immediately (e.g., will it make them lose control and restraint?), in the near future (e.g., will it make them feel sick tomorrow morning?), and in the long term (e.g., if they add drinking alcohol into their lifestyle, how will it change their lives?). That uncertainty can be scary. We face similar feelings with the prospect of changing and improving our mindsets.

Here are some suggestions that may help you in letting go.

First, learn about people who have changed and improved their mindsets. Carol Dweck's book *Mindset* possesses many examples. One student, Tony, changed his internal monologue after learning about fixed and growth mindsets. He went from "I am naturally gifted; I don't need to study; I don't need to sleep; I'm superior" to "Don't worry so much about being smart. Don't worry so much about avoiding failures. That becomes self-destructive. Let's start to study and sleep and get on with life."

Second, seek out little wins. What skill do you want to possess that shouldn't take significant effort? For example, if you want to learn to bake a cake, watch a few YouTube videos and practice making one cake every weekend for two months. By the end, you will learn that developing a new skill is not as challenging as you anticipated. The surprising reality according to Josh Kaufman, the author of *The First 20 Hours: How to Learn Anything...Fast*, is that while trying something new can be challenging, "The human brain is optimized to pick up new skills extremely quickly. If you persist and practice in an intelligent way, you'll always experience dramatic improvements in a very short period of time...You can usually achieve the goals you set for yourself in around 20 hours of deliberate practice."

Third, engage in positive self-talk. In a massive study involving over 44,000 people, a team of sports psychologists tested three motivational techniques to see which had the most positive effects: self-talk (saying to yourself, "I can do better"), imagery (imagining yourself doing something better), and if-then planning (e.g., "If I start to doubt myself, then I will remind myself that I have the skills). Self-talk was found to have the most positive effects on the intensity of one's efforts and performance.

Some ways that you can use self-talk to develop more of a growth mindset include:

- Rather than say you cannot do something, add "yet" to the end of that sentence. Instead of saying, "I cannot bake a cake from scratch," say, "I cannot bake a cake from scratch yet."
- Simply replace the words *failing* or *struggling* with *learning*.
- Instead of thinking, "This is hard" or "I can't do it," try thinking, "I can always improve, so I'll keep trying."

I recently engaged in this. As an academic and researcher, I am expected to publish my research in top academic journals, where the acceptance rates hover around 10 percent. Failure is not uncommon. Nonetheless, that doesn't make rejection any easier. When a journal rejected a research paper I thought was really good, my brain started sending me fixed mindset messages: "You aren't a good researcher," "You don't have what it takes to get published," and "You should probably give up on this paper, because you are likely to only see more rejection moving forward."

Thankfully, because I know the cues of a fixed mindset, I was able to counteract these natural feelings. I did so in a couple of ways. First, I told myself that this was an opportunity to learn, grow, and improve my paper. Second, I reminded myself that my dissertation was soundly rejected from five academic journals before it was picked up by a sixth. And, about a year after its release, I was informed that my paper won the journal's award for being the best paper published for that year.

Through self-talk, I was able to go from feeling defeated and hopeless to possessing a much more positive and excited approach to improving the paper and submitting it to a new journal.

Other ideas include:

- Redefine *genius* to being something that comes from hard work and not talent alone.
- Disassociate criticism from failure, and see criticism as an opportunity to learn and improve.
- See challenges similar to weight training, resistance will make you stronger and more capable of taking on challenges in the future.
- Become more realistic about the time it takes to learn a new skill (fixed mindset individuals overestimate the time it takes to develop a new skill and thus get frustrated faster).

Remember: cultivating a growth mindset could be the single most important thing you ever do to help you achieve success. I hope you will put in the intentional and concerted effort to develop more of a growth mindset to enhance not only your thinking, learning, and behavior but also your success in life, work, and leadership.

PART III
OPEN MINDSET

Chapter 9
DISCOVERING AN OPEN MINDSET

The rate at which you learn and progress in the world depends on how willing you are to weigh the merit of new ideas, even if you don't instinctively like them. Perhaps especially if you don't like them.
—Shane Parrish

Ray Dalio is the founder of Bridgewater Associates. Under his leadership, Bridgewater has become the world's largest hedge fund ($160 billion in assets under management), making more money for its clients than any other hedge fund in history. In 2016, *Fortune* recognized Bridgewater as the fifth most important private company in the United States.

What has been their secret to success?

In his book *Principles*, Dalio reveals his secret. It is what he calls "radical open-mindedness." To Dalio, radical open-mindedness combines always seeking radical truth with possessing radical transparency. He and his team practice this to such a degree that all of their meetings are video-recorded, they developed baseball cards for each employee to help them engage in more effective decision-making, and they created a system that allows employees to rate how believable someone is in real time to help enhance feedback and development. This culture even allows for lower-level employees to provide constructive criticism to their leaders in an effort to improve the organization.

After a meeting one day, Dalio received the following email from a lower-level employee:

> Ray—you deserve a "D–" for your performance today in the ABC meeting and everyone that was in the room that saw you agrees on that harsh assessment (give or take half a grade). This was especially disappointing for two reasons: 1) You have been great in previous meetings where the subject matter to be covered was the same, and 2) We held a specific planning meeting yesterday to ask you to focus tightly on culture and portfolio structuring because we had only 2 hours to have you cover those two topics, me cover the investment process, have Greg do the observatory and have Randal do implementation. Instead, you took a total of 62 minutes (I measured) but worse, you rambled for 50 minutes on what I think was portfolio structuring topics and only then got to culture and you talked about that for 12 minutes. It was obvious to all of us that you did not prepare at all because there is no way you could have been that disorganized at the outset if you had prepared.

How would you respond to an email like this? Here is what Dalio did: he forwarded it to all employees, thankful for the direct feedback that would lead to improvement, and in an effort to reinforce and encourage the idea that radical truth, transparency, and open-mindedness at all levels of the organization is vital for progress and improvement.

While Dalio continually strives to be open-minded and has built that culture into Bridgewater, he was not always that way.

The Journey to Radical Open-Mindedness

Dalio founded Bridgewater Associates in 1975. By the end of the decade, he was a respectable voice in the investment community. Because of his knowledge of various commodities markets (e.g., grains, livestock, meats), his consulting advice for McDonald's led to the development of Chicken McNuggets, one of the most successful fast-food menu items ever.

From 1979 to 1981, Dalio and Bridgewater navigated one of the most volatile periods ever for the markets. In 1981, economic issues were coming to a head. Not only was inflation at 10 percent and increasing, but economic activity was continuing to slow. Debts were rising faster than borrowers' incomes. On top of this, American banks were lending huge amounts to emerging countries, often much more than their operating capital.

Seeing this, Dalio wrote a controversial article to his clients in March 1981, predicting a severe depression. In it, he stated, "The enormity of our debt implies that the depression will be as bad or worse than that witnessed in the thirties."

In August 1982, Mexico defaulted on its debt. It became clear that other emerging countries were also going to default, too. The banks that lent money to these countries had no choice but to shut down loan activity—essentially what Dalio had predicted 18 months earlier.

Since he was one of the few people who correctly pegged what was happening in the markets, he started to get a lot of attention, appearing on TV and testifying before Congress. In these appearances, he confidently declared we were headed for depression and explained why. He put the odds of another great depression at 95%, with the only other alternative being hyperinflation. He also invested his capital accordingly, protecting himself against worst-case scenarios.

This time, Dalio ended up being dead wrong. Not only did the markets hold, rather than crash, but they rocketed upward. This led to the 1980s being labeled as the "roaring eighties," as the US economy enjoyed the greatest noninflationary growth period in its history.

Unfortunately for Dalio and Bridgewater, his certainty in an economic collapse and the performance of the investments he had based on that certainty resulted in Bridgewater losing so much money that eventually he had to let everyone go, even his best friend and partner. He lost so much money that he had to borrow $4,000 from his dad until he could sell his family's second car. He found himself scrambling to support his wife and two young children.

Of this experience, Dalio writes:

My experience over this period was like a series of blows to the head with a baseball bat. Being so wrong—and especially so publicly wrong—was incredibly humbling and cost me just about everything I had built at Bridgewater. I saw that I had been an arrogant jerk who was totally confident in a totally incorrect view...I had been wildly overconfident and had let my emotions get the better of me. I am still shocked and embarrassed by how arrogant I was.

This was a turning point in Dalio's life in many ways, including his most foundational level: his mindset. He said that he knew that if he didn't want to experience such a disaster again, he would need to change his "mindset from thinking 'I'm right' to asking myself 'How do I know I'm right?'"—in other words, changing from a closed to open mindset.

Through this experience, Dalio came to value radical open-mindedness and infused that into the culture of Bridgewater. Dalio says, "In retrospect, my crash was one of the best things that ever happened to me because it gave me the humility I needed to balance my aggressiveness." This change in mindset became a foundational driver in Bridgewater's success and growth from a one-man organization on life support in the early 1980s to the largest hedge fund in the United States.

Open and Closed Mindsets

Let's more fully consider the mindset shift that led Dalio and Bridgewater to become so successful.

As mentioned earlier, our mindsets fall on a continuum between negative and positive. In the case of closed and open mindsets, a closed mindset is on the negative end, while an open mindset is on the positive end. Each of us falls somewhere along this continuum.

Each mindset is driven by a different goal. When we have a closed mindset, we are primarily concerned about being right and being seen as such. We tend to think that what we know is best and therefore close our minds to the ideas and suggestions of others. We value only the information that supports and validates our ideas, while avoiding ideas that might indicate we are wrong.

When we have an open mindset, we are primarily concerned about seeking truth and thinking optimally. This desire comes with the beliefs that we have incomplete information and can be wrong. It drives us to be open to and seek out the ideas and suggestions of others to improve our current position and come closer to the truth. With this mindset, we are able to put off our ego's need to be seen as being right or having all the answers and avoid blind spots that limit the quality of our thinking and decision-making.

Where Is Your Mindset on the Continuum of Closed to Open?

Where is your mindset on the continuum of closed to open? To quote Shane Parrish, on his blog, *Farnam Street*: "Before you smugly slap an open-minded sticker on your chest, consider this: closed-minded people could never consider that they could actually be closed-minded. In fact, their perceived open-mindedness is what's so dangerous."

I don't know about you, but I can completely relate to this. If we went back a decade and you asked me if I was open-minded, I would have resoundingly said, "Yes!" But I now look back on my old self and see a closed-minded, rigid-thinking person.

When we are closed-minded, it is difficult to see how we can be more open-minded. We already think we are! This makes self-evaluating the degree of our open-mindedness very difficult. It may be why some received a score on their personal mindset assessment well above the middle of the scale (e.g., a 4.9; the middle of the scale is a 4.0) yet were given a result indicating more of a closed mindset. The reality is that it is challenging for people to self-select responses that suggest closed-mindedness. Thus, it is better to place less weight on your raw assessment score and more weight on the results indicating your standing relative to others who have completed the assessment.

Characteristics of People with Open and Closed Mindsets

The differences between those with closed and open mindsets couldn't be greater. Those with a closed mindset are likely to lead with providing answers rather than asking questions or inviting feedback or disagreement. Open mindset people are likely to lead with asking questions and continually seeking new information and diverse perspectives that will better themselves, their position, and those around them.

A classic case where open and closed mindsets commonly reveal themselves is in a debate or discussion between people on opposite ends of the political spectrum. Open-minded people can soak in the ideas of others that may differ from their own and weigh them against their own views and philosophies. The closed-minded make no such attempt to understand others' positions. They fail to weigh outside ideas against their own ideas and philosophies, often considering their own to be superior. One is primarily interested in obtaining the best point of view, while the other focuses on communicating what they consider to be the best point of view.

Interestingly, researchers from the University of Southern California investigated this political closed-mindedness at a neural level. Using magnetic resonance imaging (MRI), the researchers found that when individuals identify strongly with one political point of view and are presented with information supporting the other side, their brains literally shut down to protect their egoic identity. Individuals who adhere to a certain political philosophy but do not strongly identify with it can entertain ideas that differ from their own.

The differences between mindsets do not stop there. To help you better evaluate the mindset you possess, let's more fully compare and contrast the differences:

People with a Closed Mindset:	People with an Open Mindset:
Stubbornly and illogically hold on to their own point of view	Are open to the possibility that they could be wrong
Prefer to listen to ideas that support their own thoughts and opinions	Seek out ideas that disconfirm their own thoughts and opinions
Are primarily concerned with validating their perspective	Have a genuine fear of missing important perspectives
Are quick to judge	Are willing to suspend judgment for a time to properly evaluate another point of view

Tend to lead with their best thinking without exploring different points of view	Seek to explore different points of view to ensure that they are seeing themselves, others, and their situation as accurately as possible
Are confident that they have the best answers	Recognize that they likely have not taken in all relevant information
Are prone to give answers	Are prone to ask questions
Have a tendency to presume and be assertive with their presumptions	Have a tendency to ask to ensure their presumptions are accurate
Do not seek to understand what others are thinking and are thus out of touch with how other people see things	Seek to understand what others are thinking and are thus in touch with how other people see things
Primarily want to be told that what they are doing is the right course of action	Want to find out if they or others are doing something wrong or is standing in the way of achieving their goals
Avoid criticism or, if they receive criticism, get defensive and/or are quick to justify it away	Welcome criticism and seek to learn from it without getting defensive
Do not actively seek out feedback	Actively seek out feedback
Are willing to fight to demonstrate they are right	Are willing to fight to find out what is true
See being right as being a winner and being wrong as being a loser	See getting the decision right as being the winner (even if it means changing your thinking) and getting the decision wrong as being the loser
Are unwilling to have their ideas challenged and become frustrated when they are	Are willing to have their ideas challenged and become curious when they are
Directly or indirectly discourage others from telling them when they could be wrong	Encourage others to tell them when they could be wrong

See disagreements as threats	See disagreements as opportunities for learning
Block others from speaking and do not leave space for others to express their thoughts and ideas	Are often more interested in listening than speaking and encourage others to express their thoughts and ideas
Cannot hold two opposing thoughts, views, or concepts simultaneously in their minds	Can hold two opposing thoughts, views, or concepts simultaneously in their minds, and are able to go back and forth between them to assess their relative merits
Are typically uncomfortable being around those who know a lot more than they do	Are thrilled to be around people who know more than they do

As you continue to self-evaluate and awaken to the degree of your open-mindedness, keep these lessons from my personal research in mind:

1. When individuals assess their own mindset, they have a tendency to overweight the times that they are open and underweight the times that they are closed.
2. When individuals assess the mindset of others, they have a tendency to overweight the times they are closed and underweight the times that they are open.

Even though you likely recognize that you have a closed mindset at times, you are quick to identify instances where you express an open mindset, which likely leads you to believe that you are more open than is actually the case. This also means that even when you demonstrate closed-mindedness only in a few instances, those are enough to lead others to perceive you as closed-minded. It is important to recognize that those with whom we live, work, and associate expect us to be a person described by the right side of the table (i.e., open-minded). When we act anything less than that (i.e., closed-minded), even for a brief period, we negatively affect their perceptions of us and the culture around us. So, no matter how open-minded we think we are, chances are good that our colleagues, associates, and friends feel we could possess and they could benefit from us having an even more open mindset.

Why Do People Develop Closed Mindsets?

If having an open mindset is so beneficial, why do people ever develop a closed mindset in the first place?

There are two primary reasons, likely intertwined. The first concerns our ego. Each of us intrinsically wants to be valued by others, to have an impact, and to protect ourselves and our current status and position. This is natural, and it's often a good thing. Unfortunately, our ego continually tells us that the way we become valued, have an impact, and protect ourselves is by being on top and superior. Our ego equates giving answers with superiority, and receiving answers and asking questions with inferiority. Even when we are ignorant on a topic, our ego leads us to believe that we know enough to provide answers, and do not need to ask questions. Our ego wants us to believe that open-mindedness is a sign of weakness. Thus, our ego is continually pulling us in a closed-minded direction.

The second reason is that being closed-minded is easier—or so we tell ourselves. It can be easily argued that closed-mindedness is more efficient. Since gathering information takes valuable time and could slow down the decision process, it is easy to justify our closed-mindedness by jumping to a decision to save time. The tradeoff comes when we consider the difference between moving quickly versus the quality of our decisions and their long-term ramifications. For example, shutting down someone's idea may allow a team to move more quickly, but the cost of doing so may lead that individual to become disengaged or reluctant to speak up again, which will hurt longer-term efficiency and effectiveness.

Despite the pull of our ego and the enticement of speed and efficiency, it is important to remember that what leads to success is sometimes not what is best for us in the moment. What leads to success is the pursuit of accuracy, clarity, and truth, which ultimately leads to us identify the best answers and making the best decisions.

Stiff Back, Soft Front

You might be wondering if I'm suggesting that we should be pushovers and never take a stance.

Not at all. Having an open mindset does not mean expressing beliefs not your own or blindly accepting other people's conclusions. It does not prevent us from having a stiff back, but it does mean that we can also have a soft front. Thus, even when we take a stand, we can be simultaneously open to the possibility there is much that we do not know, allowing us to more fully see the perspective of others.

Isn't this idea of having a soft front just another way of describing humility? A humble person is willing to take the thoughts and ideas of others seriously, regardless of their position or level of knowledge. Those who are truly humble and willing to take the ideas of others seriously operate with a high level of self-esteem. They feel good about who they are, do not see others' different perspectives as a threat to who they are, and do not get defensive. They are able to esteem others, regardless of their perspective. Humility is a healthy and positive form of personal power that endears others to us, driven by the degree to which we have an open mindset.

Consider this quote from Ray Dalio:

> You, like me, probably don't know everything you need to know and would be wise to embrace that fact. If you can think for yourself while being open-minded in a clearheaded way to find out what is best for you to do, and if you can summon up the courage to do it, you will make the most of your life. If you can't do that, you should reflect on why that is, because that's most likely your greatest impediment to getting more of what you want out of life.

This leads to the deeper role our closed and open mindsets play in our thinking, learning, and behavior.

Chapter 10

HOW OPEN MINDSETS DRIVE
THINKING, LEARNING, AND BEHAVIOR

*Keep your mind open to change all the time. Welcome it. Court it. It is
only by examining and reexamining your opinions and ideas that you
can progress.*

—Dale Carnegie

I n the 1840s, hospitals in Vienna faced a mysterious, terrifying epidemic of
childbed (puerperal) fever, which caused the deaths of about 15 percent of
new mothers who had just delivered babies. At the epidemic's peak, one-
third of the women died in or shortly after labor, three times the mortality rate
of those attended by midwives. To try to arrive at an explanation, a Hungarian
physician named Ignaz Semmelweis came up with a hypothesis. He observed
that the doctors and medical students who attended the women were going
straight to the delivery room from performing autopsies on the women who
had died the day before. Though no one understood the concept of germs or
hospital-borne viruses at the time, Semmelweis thought they might be carrying
a "morbid poison" on their hands. Therefore, he instructed his students to wash
their hands in a chlorine antiseptic solution before going to the maternity ward.

Low and behold, the women stopped dying—an astonishing, lifesaving outcome.

Yet, when Semmelweis tried to teach other doctors about the value of washing their hands, they refused to accept the evidence and essentially told him to get lost.

There was Ignaz Semmelweis, giving his colleagues advice that would make them better doctors and help them save dozens, if not hundreds, of lives. Which it did. A no-brainer, right? Yet, the doctors remained closed-minded.

Why didn't Semmelweis's colleagues accept the evidence and even thank him effusively for finding the reason for the tragic, unnecessary deaths of their patients?

Answer: their egos.

In order for the physicians to accept his simple lifesaving intervention, they would have to admit that they had helped cause the deaths of many women in their care. This intolerable realization went straight to the heart of the physicians' view of themselves as medical experts and wise healers. They wanted to be seen as being right more than they wanted truth.

Don't you find it interesting that so many of the world's greatest breakthroughs are met with so much resistance? Such resistance is surely limiting, if not detrimental, for the individuals affected and even for the world at large. At its root, it is driven by people with closed mindsets.

In his book *Principles*, Dalio clearly lays out why Bridgewater Associates promotes and espouses radical open-mindedness by clearly and forcefully discussing the consequences of not being open-minded. These include:

- Missing out on all sorts of wonderful possibilities and dangerous threats that other people might be showing you.
- Blocking criticism that could be constructive and even lifesaving.
- Losing because you stubbornly refused to learn something that would have allowed you to perform better.
- Failing to rectify bad or off-base opinions because you failed to objectively look at your situation and weigh what you and others think about it.

Look at the words starting each bullet point: *missing, blocking, losing,* and *failing.* Do those describe an individual who is thinking, learning, and behaving in a success-driven way? Of course not. Altogether, Dalio writes,

> Holding wrong opinions in one's head and making bad decisions based on them instead of having thoughtful disagreements is one of the greatest tragedies of mankind. Being able to thoughtfully disagree [can] so easily lead to radically improved decision making in all areas—public policy, politics, medicine, science, philanthropy, personal relationships, and more.

Let's explore in greater depth how our closed and open mindsets influence our thinking, learning, and behavior.

Thinking and Learning

The movie *Hidden Figures* is based on a true story involving the lives and challenges of three brilliant African American women at NASA who were the brains behind one of the greatest operations in history: the launch of astronaut John Glenn into orbit. Each of these women played a different role at NASA.

Katherine Johnson (played by Taraji P. Henson) is a mathematician who is brought into the team responsible for figuring out the launch windows, trajectories, and return paths for the rockets and their astronauts heading to space and back. She stands out among her team for three reasons: she is brilliant, female, and black.

Katherine's direct supervisor, Paul Stafford (played by Jim Parsons), is a character created to be a composite of a number of engineers with whom she worked. Throughout the movie, Paul is seen limiting Katherine's access to information and meetings vital to her performing her job, all because she is female and black. Despite these limitations, Katherine continually finds a way to excel, proving herself among the best and the brightest at NASA.

Al Harrison (played by Kevin Costner), another composite character, is the head of the Space Task Group and Paul Stafford's boss. Al recognizes the value that Katherine brings to the group, and he also becomes increasingly aware of Paul's attempts to limit Katherine.

In one particular scene, Al sees Katherine and Paul in a heated conversation:

AL HARRISON: Paul, what's happening here?

KATHERINE JOHNSON: Mr. Harrison, I would like to attend today's briefing.

AL HARRISON: And why is that?

KATHERINE JOHNSON: Well, sir, the data changes so fast, the capsule changes, the weight and the landing zones are all changing every day. I do my work, you attend these briefings, I have to start over. Colonel Glenn launches in a few weeks, we don't have the math figured out yet.

AL HARRISON *(to Paul)*: And why is it she can't attend?

PAUL STAFFORD: Because she doesn't have clearance, Al.

KATHERINE JOHNSON: I cannot do my work effectively if I do not have all of the data and all of the information as soon as it's available. I need to be in that room hearing what you hear.

PAUL STAFFORD: Pentagon briefings are not for civilians. It requires the highest clearance.

KATHERINE JOHNSON: I feel like I'm the best person to present my calculation.

AL HARRISON: You're not going to let this go, are you?

KATHERINE JOHNSON: No, I am not.

PAUL STAFFORD: And she is a woman. There is no protocol for a woman to attend these meetings.

AL HARRISON: Okay, I get that part, Paul. But within these walls who, uh, who makes the rules?

KATHERINE JOHNSON: You, sir, you are the boss. You just have to act like one, sir.

Later in the film, Al says to Paul: "You know what your job is, Paul? Find the genius among those geniuses, to pull us all up. We all get to the peak together or we don't get there at all." This inspiring lesson is designed to get Paul to look past his biases and do what is best for the team, which involves allowing Katherine to play a bigger role in the team instead of limiting her because he was not comfortable with her gender or skin color.

By closing himself off to Katherine, including her abilities and her voice, Paul was limiting the speed at which the team could solve problems and, therefore, how quickly NASA could get a rocket into space.

This example plays out in our workplaces, service groups, and families all the time. In fact, I would venture to guess that for any group that you are a part of, you can identify someone who, because of their closed mindset, is limiting the flow of ideas, the speed of progress, and the group's overall ability to excel. Depending upon your mindset, it might be you.

Those who play this role, like Paul, feel justified in their position. They like stability and certainty, which is a nice way of saying that they are fearful of change and people or things that are different from them. They see themselves as protectors. But being the protector does not mean that we need to have a hard front, where we close ourselves off to available information, prematurely dismiss relevant information, and are unwilling to change our minds in light of new ideas. Remember, an open mindset means that while we may have a stiff back, we can also have a soft front. Having a soft front means that we are open to available information, avoid prematurely dismissing relevant information, and are willing to change our mindsets in light of new ideas.

Out of these two options, who do you think is going to be a better thinker, decision maker, and learner? Who do you think is going to be agile and more willing to adapt to changing market conditions? Who is going to keep pace with the rate of change? Who is going to be left in the dust?

If that wasn't enough to convince you of the value of an open mindset for thinking and learning, researchers have repeatedly found that those with an open mindset are more impartial, less biased, and more accurate in their processing and decision-making. Let me give you two examples.

First, consider situations where you have been faced with a difficult decision between competing options. Once you made a decision, how did you view the options that you did not select? Researchers Eddie Harmon-Jones and Cindy Harmon-Jones found that those with a closed mindset tend to view the alternative options much more negatively than those with an open mindset. Essentially, they can be struggling between multiple options at one moment, but immediately after making a decision, their selected option magically becomes substantially better than the alternatives, taking a rather extreme position. It is as if those with a closed mindset do not want to feel mentally conflicted about their decision. Those with an open mindset, on the other hand, are able to be much more authentic about their decision-making process. In all, those with a closed mindset are more inclined to be biased about the value of the decisions they make, leaving them vulnerable to sticking with a failing course of action.

Second, multiple research teams have found that those with open mindsets are much more accurate judges of their true contribution to their success. Based upon what we know about Lee Iacocca, all signs point to him also having a closed mindset. This is revealed by how he confidently portrayed himself as the savior of Chrysler. In his mind, it was he, not market conditions, that led to Chrysler's success. Yet, a closer depiction of reality is that Lee Iacocca was only one piece in a larger puzzle that contributed to Chrysler's uptick in success during the first half of his tenure as CEO. Individuals with open mindsets are much more inclined to recognize the factors beyond themselves that contribute to success. Findings like these have led researchers to assert that those with closed mindsets are much more prone to illusions of invulnerability and less accurately perceive their probabilities for success, which together can be a recipe for disaster.

Altogether, the evidence seems clear: we make better decisions and solve problems more effectively if we operate with an open mindset and are willing to consider the possibilities that we do not have all the information or right answers and that others might see something better than us. Just think of all of the lives that could have been saved had Ignaz Semmelweis's colleagues listened to him sooner. Dalio summarized this basic idea well when he wrote, "The more open-minded you are, the less likely you are to deceive yourself."

Behaviors

An open mindset leads to better thinking and greater learning. But when it comes to the impact on our behaviors, there is evidence of a tradeoff.

When we believe that we can be wrong and want to ensure that we are thinking optimally, we open ourselves up to exploring alternatives and new information. As you might imagine, taking the time to explore alternatives and new information can be time-consuming. But when we believe that we are right and know the best direction, rather than spend time seeking out alternative perspectives, we become much more action-oriented and persistent, often in an effort to confirm our thinking and decision-making. Thus, it appears that there is a tradeoff between taking action and ensuring one is headed in the right direction.

However, I am not sure that it is helpful to think about these mindsets as an either/or scenario. To demonstrate, consider David Goggins.

In his book, *Can't Hurt Me*, David Goggins presents his incredible life story. He takes you on his journey from being a severely abused child, to uneducated teenager, to Air Force flame out, to 300-pound exterminator, to 195-pound Navy SEAL who made it through three Hell Weeks, to Army Ranger, to ultra-runner and triathlete. The book is a fantastic portrayal of someone improving one's mindsets to become more successful. But that doesn't mean that he improved in all of his mindsets. As Goggins changed his mindsets, he went from lacking clarity and direction to becoming someone who could accomplish anything that he put his mind to. But, as he improved is ability to accomplish anything he put his mind to, he further entrenched his closed mindset.

This was exposed to his detriment during his Navy SEAL career, when he was seeking to get invited to test for SEAL Team 6, which contains the very best Navy SEALs and is the United States' most elite antiterrorism unit. In order to be invited to test for SEAL Team 6, one must have five years of experience as a SEAL. Approaching his five-year mark, and with his goal to receive an invitation to SEAL Team 6, Goggins was "locked in" and pushing himself in all areas of his life. When he was in training mode, he was exerting maximum effort. When his team was off for the evening or for the weekend, he was studying or improving his physical fitness. He was also looking at his fellow SEALs with contempt because they didn't seem to be putting forth as much time and effort as he was. Instead, they would regularly socialize with each other on the evenings and weekends. He justified the growing distance between himself and his teammates as being the "uncommon amongst uncommon."

Seeing this growing distance, his commanding officers recommended that he try harder to fit in socially with his team. While his desire to enhance his skills as a SEAL was commendable, it was also important that his teammates trust him, particularly if they had to go into battle. They pointed out that by isolating himself, he was preventing trust from being built.

Because Goggins was too focused on getting ready for the tests associated with the selection process for SEAL Team 6, he was closed to the suggestion to connect better with his teammates. Ultimately, because he was unable to open himself to the feedback of his commanding officer, he was not invited try out for SEAL Team 6, which stalled his career.

It is fair to say that his closed mindset played a role in allowing him to lock into and accomplish some incredible feats, truly making himself an "uncommon amongst uncommon." But it is also fair to say that his closed mindset prevented him from engaging in behaviors that could have allowed him to accomplish a goal that was really important to him.

It is possible to both desire to think optimally and take disciplined and focused action. It would have taken relatively little effort and compromise for Goggins to engage in behaviors to build trust with his team, and it likely would not have had any bearing upon how he would have performed had he been invited to test for SEAL Team 6.

Summary

How do these ideas come together? Let's compare Alan, the leader of the nonprofit organization, to Ray Dalio, and how they each approached a similar situation differently.

One time, Alan hired an employee, Tanya, to focus on building revenues by selling the training services that Alan and other trainers could provide. This hire came at a time where other employees in the office were overwhelmed, so Alan had Tanya step away from sales to help with other logistical and administrative issues. The other employees came to rely upon Tanya, continually pulling her into their work and away from sales, her focal responsibility. While Alan initially wasn't fully aware of this, he did seem to like that the office staff seemed to be running much more efficiently. Over time, though, he became concerned that Tanya was not making any sales. Frustrated by this, Alan strongly considered firing her on the grounds that she was not doing what she was hired to do.

At this point, Alan pulled me aside, explained his desire to fire Tanya, and asked for my advice. Knowing a little about Tanya's situation, I told Alan to consider that, while Tanya hadn't made many sales, her contributions to the organization were many and positive. I even suggested that if Alan wanted her to make more sales, he would have to change his management style and prevent her from being sucked into other peoples' work, set clearer sales goals and performance objectives, and give her more developmental feedback. It was my opinion that Alan needed to give her a chance to prove herself as a salesperson before firing her.

Alan's egoic and closed mindset failed to let him see that his lack of effective management was the primary issue, not Tanya's job performance. So, rather than change how he operated, Alan was planning to fire her, until a staff member quit shortly thereafter, thus requiring Tanya to fill in more permanently on administrative duties.

Ray Dalio, on the other hand, took an open-minded approach to a frustrating situation, which ultimately resulted in positive changes for the organization.

On one occasion, a Bridgewater employee forgot to invest a client's money in a particular investment in a timely manner. The lapse cost the client several hundred thousand dollars. Dalio said that, with a closed mindset, he might have been inclined to do something dramatic, such as fire the employee—thus setting a tone that mistakes would not be tolerated. But, as he wrote, "Mistakes happen all the time, that would have only encouraged other people to hide theirs, which would have led to even bigger and more costly errors. I believed strongly that we should bring problems and disagreements to the surface to learn what should be done to make things better."

Rather than discipline this employee, he worked with them to develop an error log. From that time forward, when mistakes were made in the trading department, they would be logged, allowing for follow-up and improvement.

This enhanced Bridgewater's open-mindedness and ability to learn, evolve, and improve.

Because of Dalio's open mindset, he was able to see this costly mistake as an opportunity to learn and to respond positively by creating a system that would allow the organization to continually learn and refine their systems to serve their clients more effectively.

Chapter 11

THE POWER OF OPEN MINDSETS TO DRIVE SUCCESS IN LIFE, WORK, AND LEADERSHIP

Those who cannot change their minds cannot change anything.
—**George Bernard Shaw**

T he movie *Pitch Perfect* focuses on an all-female collegiate a capella singing group as they pursue their goal of winning the collegiate national championship (after choking, quite literally, the year before). Three of the main characters are Aubrey (played by Anna Camp), a senior and closed-minded authoritative leader of the group; Beca (played by Anna Kendrick), a freshman with innovative ideas on how to mash together music from different genres to create really interesting arrangements; and Chloe (played by Brittany Snow), who had vocal surgery and can no longer hit high notes.

In one scene, there is frustration because Chloe can no longer hit a particular note, and they are forced to choose someone to replace Chloe for her solo. Chloe nominates Beca:

CHLOE: I think Beca should take my solo…

BECA: …I would be happy to [solo] if got to pick a new song and do an arrangement.

AUBREY: Well, that is not how we run things here.

CHLOE: Aubrey, maybe Beca has a point. Maybe we can try something new— *(cut off by Aubrey)*

AUBREY: Acca-scuse me. You can sing "Turn the Beat Around," and that's the last I want to hear of this.

BECA: That song is tired. We won't win with that song. Look, if we pulled samples from different genres and layer them together— *(cut off by Aubrey)*

AUBREY: Okay, let me explain this to you because you still don't seem to get it. Our goal is to get back to the finals. These songs will get us there. So excuse me if I don't take advice from some alt girl with her Mad Lib beats when she's never even been in a competition. Have I made myself clear?

Aubrey sees herself as the experienced leader who knows what it takes for the group to be successful. Yet, her closed mindset causes her to get defensive and shut down Beca's suggestion for doing something innovative. In fact, because of Aubrey's closed-mindedness and need to be seen as being right, Beca leaves the group. After a period of time, the group realizes Beca's talent adds value to the group. She comes back, and with her help, they win the collegiate national championship.

While *Pitch Perfect* is fictional, I do not think interactions like this are uncommon. Some examples include parents who fail to listen to their children and instead respond by saying, "Because I am you mother, that's why!" Perhaps someone gets defensive after receiving constructive criticism from their spouse instead of trying to see their own blind spots. Or managers are quick to shoot down the ideas and suggestions of their teams. This leaves me wondering how many times we pass up ideas that will make us more successful because we are too stubborn and closed-minded to see that our way of thinking and doing things could be improved.

Our closed/open mindsets play a most significant role in our lives: they impact the quality of our decisions. We must recognize that our success is based upon our effectiveness in decision-making. In *The Noticer Returns*, Andy Andrews writes, "A person's long-term level of success or failure—as an employee, a manager, or an owner—in any part of business will be greatly determined by the quality and accuracy of his decisions." Andrews goes on to suggest that if we can make better decisions, we will engage in better actions, produce better results, enhance our reputation, and ultimately drive success across our life, work, and leadership.

Success in Life

While there are a variety of ways having an open mindset enhances our success in our life, I want to focus on two foundational elements of a fulfilling life: the quality of our relationships with others and our decision-making.

Quality of Our Relationships

Do you know anyone who acts as though they know it all, always needs to be right, and seems unwilling to listen to alternative points of view? My guess is that more than one person comes to mind. Where do these people rank on your list of people you want to spend time with? For most, they are at the bottom of our list.

Fortunately, the percentage of people who fit the description above is small. The majority of closed-minded people actually fit a different mold, but the effects of their closed-mindedness still paint a picture of being unapproachable and off-putting.

Three common types of closed-mindedness plague the majority of closed-minded people. It is important to point out that people who are closed-minded in these different ways are not closed-minded 100% of the time, but even a small degree of closed-mindedness paints us as a closed-minded person in the eyes of others. Thus, it is important to be aware of these three forms of closed-mindedness and be sensitive to the degree that we fall into each.

The first common type of closed-mindedness is when people consider themselves to be such experts that they do not create space for others with less expertise to have ideas and suggestions. The second common type involves those whom I call conscientious thinkers. They are thorough, responsible, organized, and they like to think things through to come up with a direction or solution well in advance. Being ahead of others in the decision-making process causes them to perceive others' ideas as being "behind the times," and therefore, they are quick to dismiss those ideas. The third common type concerns those focused on personal or professional attainment. Think David Goggins. They have already come to a decision about what needs to be done and now are focused on implementing that decision. When people are in implementation mode, they see new ideas as obstacles to their pace and their decision-making. When we step back and consider why people commonly fall into one of these closed-minded types, an interesting pattern emerges. At the core, these types of closed-mindedness are founded upon two barriers: ego and blind spots. The closed-minded individual wants to be right, or at least be seen as being right. This is the ego barrier. The blind spot barrier occurs when the individual believes they can see everything of importance and fails to acknowledge that there are other perspectives invisible to them that might be essential for making high-quality decisions.

These barriers prevent open-mindedness and get in the way of building quality relationships.

Let me give you a personal example to demonstrate how this plays out. When I worked for Gallup, I was placed into a customer engagement project that was deep into implementation mode. I was brought in to do some deep-dive analyses on the customer engagement data.

The project was managed primarily by the partner on the account and informally by the partner's mentor, both people I hadn't worked with previously. Both considered themselves experts on the topic. Because they designed the data collection methodology for the customer engagement data, they had already thought through a variety of decision points. They checked the boxes for the three closed-minded types: conscientious experts in implementation mode.

Prior to doing my analyses, I learned that we collected data from customers in two different ways. Some responded to an online survey, while others took an in-store survey. When I did my analyses, I looked at the results not just across the entire data set but also based upon how the data was collected, to see if there was a meaningful difference based upon data collection methods.

Sure enough, the results differed significantly between the online and in-store data. This concerned me, because we were going to present recommendations to the client based upon our results, and unfortunately, we effectively had three different results: online survey, in-store survey, and blended results. To me, this was a big problem and a lose-lose situation. I brought this issue to the attention of the partner and his mentor, both of whom immediately dismissed my concerns and failed to take them seriously.

After getting off the phone, I was not frustrated with the decision they made, but I was frustrated my voice wasn't taken seriously or respected. In turn, this affected the degree to which I respected those men as leaders and the degree to which I wanted to work with them moving forward.

Although the context was ripe for closed-mindedness, I could clearly see both the ego and blind spot barriers driving their closed-mindedness. First, since they designed a flawed data collection effort, had they taken me seriously, they would have been forced to admit they had made a mistake. Surely a blow to their egos. Second, both knew they had a better perspective on the project than I, which likely led them to think that they could see everything. However, they had not reviewed the deep-level analyses I conducted and how different each set of results was. While they could see much, they were blind to new information that might ultimately limit the effectiveness of the recommendations they ultimately provided to the client.

As someone who has been not only on the receiving end of these forms of closed-mindedness but also guilty of all of these forms of closed-mindedness, I have learned that two consequences occur that affect our relationships with others. First, when someone's ideas are shut down without validation, they do not feel valued. Second, they no longer feel safe putting forward ideas or suggestions in the future, putting a limit on the quality of the relationship.

Quality of Our Decision-Making

How many conscious decisions does an adult make per day? A hundred? A thousand? Even more? Believe it or not, researchers put the number at 35,000. That's more than 20 decisions every minute of every day. While the vast majority are small decisions, it goes to show that if we improve our decision-making, even incrementally, its impact will quickly add up.

Think about the big decisions you have made: whether or not to go to college, where to go to college, and what to major in; what job to take; who to marry; whether or not to have children; whether to take a new job opportunity. We can keep going. These decisions have greatly impacted our lives to date. As you think about these decisions, consider the mindset you possessed at the time. Did it guide you to seek the opinions of others? Who? How many? Were these people who would confirm your interests or provide a unique or different perspective, even testing and challenging your ideas? Did you resist the ideas of others, thinking, "I can go this alone"? Did you fear missing important perspectives?

Now for the kicker: if your mindset was more open when you made any of these decisions, would you have made different, better choices?

If you are like me, it may be hard to imagine your life any other way. However, the reality is that I largely stumbled through some of these decisions without thinking too much about them. I just took what was offered. While some decisions worked for me, I can't help but wonder how my life could have been different, better, or even more successful had I not allowed my ego- and blind-spot-driven closed mindset get in the way.

An open mindset opens us up to consider more options, triangulate with more knowledgeable people, deal with our realities more effectively, and ultimately make the best possible decisions. On this topic, in his book *Principles*, Ray Dalio states, "It pays to be open-minded…Remember that the quality of the life you get will depend largely on the quality of the decisions that you make as you pursue your goals." He also adds, "If you are too proud of what you know or of how good you are at something you will learn less, make inferior decisions, and fall short of your potential."

Success in Work

In 2012, Google, on a quest to build the "perfect team," embarked on a massive research project—code-named Project Aristotle—to identify what made their top-performing teams so good. Since Google's top executives long believed that the best teams were built by simply combining the best people, they started looking at team composition involving different mixtures of talent, personality, relationships outside of work, gender and ethnic diversity, and so on. What they found through this deep dive was…nothing. No patterns showed up in their analysis.

They went back to the drawing board and reviewed the dynamics, relationships, and work habits that created their unique team cultures. This included the degree to which team members or leaders interrupted each other, conversational order, celebrating birthdays, discussing weekend plans or activities, engaging in gossip, and getting down to business. This line of research, which took over a year, produced some patterns and results. They realized that these dynamics, relationships, and habits were key to improving Google's teams, but now they had to identify which mattered most.

Through additional research, they eventually identified one primary factor central to all of Google's top-performing teams: psychological safety. This is the degree to which people within a team can feel like they can express their ideas and opinions and take risks without fear of negative repercussions. Google's top-performing teams enjoyed a culture and environment where everyone on the team felt comfortable speaking up, was open to one another's ideas, and was sensitive to the emotions and involvement of their team members.

If psychological safety leads to top team performance, then what drives psychological safety?

A necessary prerequisite is possessing an open mindset. It is only those with an open mindset that are willing to listen to and validate new ideas and suggestions, even if they are risky.

Ed Catmull, of Pixar and Disney Animation, understands the value of creating an open-minded, psychologically safe culture. He states that this culture has been foundational to their monumental success, but he has realized that creating such a culture is easier said than done. Producing innovative, creative, and wildly successful Pixar and Disney animated films requires problem solving and collaborating at a high level. Catmull recognizes that to do this, his teams need to openly share ideas, opinions, and criticisms, knowing that their decision-making is better if they can draw upon the collective knowledge and unvarnished opinions of the group.

However, strong internal and social forces often prevent this openness. These forces are founded in individuals' fears and instincts for self-preservation, including, in Catmull's words, "the fear of saying something stupid and looking bad, of offending someone or being intimidated, and of retaliating or being retaliated against." These forces increase exponentially when the environment fuels employees' desire to self-protect, such as in strong hierarchies where the stakes are high and more people are present.

How have Pixar and Disney Animation fought off the natural forces that erode psychological safety in order to create a more positive environment to solve problems and communicate effectively? By promoting candor. Candor involves both truth-telling and a lack of reserve. Catmull found that a lack of candor ultimately leads to dysfunctional environments, leading him to state: "Believe me, you don't want to be at a company where there is more candor in the hallways than in the rooms where fundamental ideas or matters of policy are being hashed out." He finds that when employees are open to candor, magic happens.

In Pixar and Disney Animation, this magic happens in "Braintrust" meetings. These meetings occur every few months to assess each movie. Their premise is simple: "Put smart, passionate people in a room together, charge them with identifying and solving problems, and encourage them to be candid with one another." These meetings start by viewing a film, or at least a portion of one, and then leaders, directors, writers, and heads of story across the organization engage in straight talk with the director. All people in the room view each other as peers (mutual respect) who are focused on improving the film and not on a hidden personal agenda, getting credit for an idea, pleasing their supervisor, or winning a point. In such an environment, incredible developmental feedback occurs, and the directors are able to be open to this feedback because they understand that everyone is trying to improve the movie, not criticize them.

Why are braintrusts so important? According to Catmull, it is because "early on, *all* of our movies suck." He goes on state:

> I'm not trying to be modest or self-effacing by saying this. Pixar films are not good at first, and our job is to make them so…This idea that all the movies we now think of as brilliant were, at one time, terrible—is a hard concept for many to grasp. But think about how easy it would be for a movie about talking toys to feel derivative, sappy, or overtly merchandise-driven. Think about how off-putting a movie about rats preparing food could be, or how risky it must've seemed to start *WALL-E* with 39

dialogue-free minutes. We dare to attempt these stories, but we don't get them right on the first pass. And this is as it should be. Creativity has to start somewhere, and we are true believers in the power of bracing, candid feedback and the iterative process—reworking, reworking, and reworking again, until a flawed story finds its throughline or a hollow character finds its soul.

Catmull has created an environment where open mindsets can thrive, despite the common organizational forces that socially incentivize closed mindsets. This has been crucial to Pixar's and Disney's animation success. By creating this environment, employees are able to:

- Seek truth, rather than to seek to be right.
- Seek to see options optimally, rather than seek to have ideas supported.
- Seek feedback, rather than avoid feedback.
- Invite new perspectives, rather than avoid new perspectives.
- See disagreement as an opportunity to learn, rather than as a threat.
- Admit they can be wrong, rather than seek to demonstrate that what they know is best.

When this happens, psychological safety flourishes, along with creativity, innovation, and effective change.

Success in Leadership

Would you prefer to follow a leader with an open mindset, someone open to the possibility of being wrong, interested in finding the best ideas, and willing to change their perspective? Or a leader with a closed mindset, who always thinks they are right, seeks to validate their personal perspective, and does not concern themselves with others' thinking? The answer seems pretty obvious, right? We would prefer to follow the humble, open-minded leader. This means that if we to be someone others want to follow, we need to become likewise.

Why is it that we like to follow humble, open-minded leaders? There is a simple explanation, one many leaders overlook. Consider the following connections: we want to follow those who value us, and we feel valued when we feel our voice and contributions are valued

I understood this before I worked for Gallup, but at Gallup, I got empirical proof. When they assess engagement within organizations, they use 12 questions or statements that they have found to be most important for driving engagement at work. Each is measured on a five-point scale, ranging from strongly disagree to strongly agree. Statements include "I know what is expected of me at work," "I have received recognition in the last seven days," and "I have a best friend at work."

While each statement is important, I was curious about which was the strongest driver of engagement. While Gallup will not publicly answer this question, I did my own personal analysis across nine organizations and almost 60,000 employees. What I found was that if an employee could strongly agree to the statement "My opinions count at work," then 95% of those employees were engaged in their job. This is a higher percentage than the rate of converted slam dunks in the NBA (89.4% during the 2017–2018 season). In other words, if employees strongly feel their opinions count at work, it is a slam dunk that they will be engaged—vigorous, dedicated, and absorbed in their work.

Getting employees to strongly agree that their opinions count is easier said than done. In Chapter 9, I mentioned most people believe they have an open mindset—whether or not that is the case. That especially holds true with leaders. Ask any person in a leadership or management position if they have an open mindset, and they are going to say yes. But, to use more of Gallup's statistics, only about 30% of employees in the United States are engaged in their jobs, which means that the majority of employees do not feel like their opinions count at work. This suggests that managers are not as open as they think they are or need to be.

Perhaps this shouldn't come as a surprise. In *Emotional Intelligence 2.0*, authors Travis Bradberry and Jean Greaves report that when you look at the emotional intelligence levels across the organization, those with the highest levels are mid-level managers. As you move up the corporate ladder, emotional intelligence dramatically decreases. Often, the executive team has the lowest levels of emotional intelligence in the organization.

In my own personal mindset research, I have begun exploring why leaders feel like they are open, yet their followers do not feel like their voice is heard. If you are a supervisor, director, manager, teacher, or parent, you might consider my findings eye-opening. If the manager demonstrates closed-mindedness on just a few occasions out of many, merely a fraction of the time, his or her employees view the manager as being closed-minded. This is similar to a 2011 *Psychology Today* article that stated it takes 10 or more repetitions of a positive statement for us to absorb it into our core beliefs, but only three seconds for a negative statement or criticism to stick. Being closed-minded, even for a minority of the time, is really off-putting to others and makes you appear as though you are unapproachable.

If you are a manager under the stress of an impending deadline and automatically shut down an idea for improvement or change, you have likely lessened others' willingness to speak up in future situations. If you are a teacher and a student challenges you in front of a class and you shut down that challenge without fully validating it, chances are your students will feel less safe coming to you in the future. If you are a parent and are inclined to shut down your children's requests with statements like "Because I am your mother/father, that's why," it is unlikely they are going to feel comfortable opening up to you about serious issues or struggles they face.

If you want to be a leader that others want to follow, effectively and positively influences others to goal achievement, and creates an environment that brings out the best of those you lead, it is essential that you possess an open mindset.

Becoming More Successful through Possessing an Open Mindset

You are going to be more successful across your life, work, and leadership with an open mindset. By acknowledging that there is much you do not know and then making yourself open to new ideas, you will be empowered to make better decisions across all facets of your life. Additionally, you will help create a psychologically safe environment, empowering others to perform at their highest levels and to work within teams most effectively. Finally, knowing that followers are sensitive to even a little closed-mindedness, you will seek to create an environment where your followers feel comfortable expressing their voice and feel as though their opinions count.

The reality is that if you are unwilling to be open to others' new ideas, perspectives, and even disagreement, you will never rise up to your potential.

Chapter 12

DEVELOPING AN OPEN MINDSET

Where there is an open mind there will always be a frontier.
—**Charles Kettering**

T he formerly closed-minded Bridgewater Associates founder, Ray Dalio, is a great example of transforming from a closed mindset to an extreme open mindset to unlock success. What led Dalio to develop such an extreme open mindset? In his words, he says,

My painful mistakes shifted me from having a perspective of "I know I'm right" to having one of "How do I know I'm right?" They gave me the humility I needed to balance my audacity. Knowing that I could be painfully wrong and curious about why other smart people saw things differently prompted me to look at things through the eyes of others as well as my own. That allowed me to see many more dimensions than if I saw things just through my own eyes. Learning how to weigh people's inputs so that I chose the best ones...increased my chances of being right and was thrilling.

Thankfully, there are other ways to develop a more open mindset than by experiencing painful mistakes.

Remember, shifting our mindsets involves changing the wiring in our brain. The best way to do this is to follow a process similar to becoming fluent at counting to 10 in a different language. But, in this instance, we need to become fluent in an open mindset. We need to get to the point where when we are presented with information that contradicts our perspective, rather than automatically shutting our brain off, we instead automatically lean into the contradiction.

To become more fluent in an open mindset, we first need to awaken to our current mindset and then take intentional regular actions to repeatedly reinforce the neural wiring associated with our open mindsets.

Awakening to Our Current Mindsets

If we are going to develop more of an open mindset, we first need to awaken to the idea that our current mindset may not be as open as we think it is.

Let me suggest several ways to arrive at a more accurate understanding of our current mindset.

First, of course, is to review the results associated with your personal mindset assessment. Subjectively assessing our personal mindsets without the right tools or frameworks can be difficult. The results of the assessment are designed to indicate your level of open-mindedness relative to thousands of others. This provides a level of objectivity that is difficult to achieve otherwise.

Second, to deepen your understanding of your mindset beyond the assessment, explore your goals and fears.

Let's start with your goals. People are driven to do what they do by adopting one of three primary goals: mastery, performing at a high level, or avoiding poor performance. The latter two goals are considered two different types of performance goals because they are focused on how they perform relative to others or some benchmark.

Consider a college student. The motivation for how they perform will be driven by their desire to learn and master the material, get a good grade (e.g., A), or avoid getting a failing grade.

If our primary goal is one of the two performance goals, it is an indicator that we may have more of a closed mindset. When our focus is on performing at a high level, we generally see entertaining new or different ideas as slowing us down or even as a signal that we are not excelling relative to others. Or, when our focus is on avoiding poor performance, we are prone to stick to the tried-and-true, be uncomfortable with ambiguity, and view suggestions and new ideas as a sign that we are failing. In both instances, we possess a closed mindset as a form of self-protection, which brings us to an even deeper way to introspect by considering our fears.

If we are not intentional about our goals and mindsets, by default, our goals and mindsets become driven by our fears. The following are fears, that if present, will lead to us unconsciously self-protect by developing a closed mindset:

- The fear of being seen as being wrong
- The fear of not being in control
- The fear of uncertainty

With each fear, we are trying to protect our ego: how we feel about ourselves and how others think about us. Consider the doctors who wouldn't listen to Ignaz Semmelweis, even though he encouraged behaviors that would allow them to save more lives. Our ego naturally tells us that our openness to others' ideas is an admission of operating ineffectively, not being enough, and not being in control.

The ego-driven fears listed above are no joke. They are often deep-seated. We must realize that if we possess those fears, we are ultimately afraid of being or appearing weak, and we tend to think that being open-minded is a form of weakness. The ironic reality, though, is that when we act upon those fears, we do appear weak. Open-mindedness and the ability to admit when we do not have all the answers is not a weakness. It is humility and vulnerability, which take great strength.

The third way to come to clarity about our current mindset is to connect with the cues associated with a closed mindset. Just as feeling film on our teeth is a cue of the state of our teeth's cleanliness, knowing and feeling the cues associated with a closed mindset can help identify our own. Some closed mindset cues include:

- Feeling defensive and/or protective
- Experiencing frustration when someone disagrees with you
- Being slow to listen and quick to say "no"
- Feeling rushed or pressured
- Being in a competition between who is right and who is wrong
- Seeking to justify feedback instead of absorbing feedback
- Thinking you know more than others in the room

Finally, talk to others about their perception of your mindset. If you can create an environment where both your loved ones and your colleagues feel comfortable giving you honest feedback, and if you are open enough to take their perspective seriously without dismissing their observations, you will likely receive information that will more fully awaken you to where you currently stand on the closed-to-open continuum.

Intentionally Reinforcing the Neural Wiring Associated with Our Open Mindsets

If you wish to shift your neural wiring to become more open-minded, here are six recommendations.

Meditate

Remember, meditation enhances our ability to shift our mindsets. It strengthens our cognitive ability to override our natural neural firings and consciously operate much more intentionally and positively.

Change Your Stories

Intertwined with our mindsets are the stories we tell ourselves. When we have a closed mindset, some of the stories we tell ourselves include:

- I know enough.
- I am right.
- I have a good perspective on this.
- I am an expert.
- They don't know what they are talking about.
- They don't have as much experience as me.

In order to become more open-minded, we have to improve our stories to include statements like:

- I can always learn more.
- I might be wrong.
- I am unable to see every facet.
- While I may know a lot, there is still much I don't know.
- Creativity requires exploring radical ideas.
- I can learn from anyone.

To improve your stories, consider times in your life when you have been really open-minded. How did you arrive at that frame of mind? Was it easy or difficult? What were the outcomes? Did you end up in a better place? What prevented you from staying in that frame of mind? Essentially, if you can remember the times you have changed your mindset without much effort and recall the positive benefits from doing so, it will help you change your story.

When asking myself these questions, I realized that I often have a closed-minded reluctance to seek direction and greater clarity from others, in all ways. The story I tell myself is that I shouldn't have to rely upon others, and that when I do, I am a burden to them and will be viewed as being needy, unintelligent, and dependent. But as I reflect upon the situations where I have asked for directions or greater clarity, rarely was I perceived in those ways. In fact, I was able to operate much more efficiently and effectively. This quick reflection helps me change my story from "asking is bad and embarrassing" to "asking is helpful and beneficial."

To help motivate you to change your stories, recall the benefits you will receive by developing more of an open mindset:

- Becoming more approachable
- Thinking more optimally
- Becoming more of a positive influence
- Becoming more creative and innovative
- Creating a more engaging living/working environment

If we can work on our stories on a regular basis, we will work out and strengthen our open mindset neural connections.

Change the Size of Your Bucket

It is helpful to draw a metaphoric comparison of your mind to a bucket. Think of a bucket as all of the information you can know about a given topic, and the water within the bucket to the level of knowledge you have on that topic.

Now, select a topic. Start with one you are an expert on. How full is your bucket?

When we have a closed mindset, we believe that our bucket is full. When water, or new knowledge, is poured into the bucket, it is not able to be captured, it overflows, and is lost.

To develop more of an open mindset, we need to change our story about the amount of available space in your bucket and allow room for new information and ideas. This means either reducing the perceived level of water currently in our bucket or opening our minds to the idea that the bucket itself might be much bigger than we originally thought.

Going from a full bucket ("I know it all") to less-than-capacity bucket ("I have yet to tap the vast potential of my knowledge and understanding") is not always easy, especially in the heat of the moment or under tight time constraints. Below are some suggestions that can help you change the size of your bucket, both holistically and in the moment.

- Holistically
  - Take time to reflect. After more emotionally charged interactions or situations, reflect upon how you handled the situation and how open you were during the "heat of the moment."
  - When making a decision, verify that you have an accurate understanding of the perspectives of all constituents.
  - Seek out ideas that disconfirm you own thoughts and opinions.
- In the moment
  - At any given moment, ask yourself, *Do I have a closed or open mindset?* Just asking yourself this question will spur you to become more open.
  - Ask yourself, *Am I seeking to be right, or am I seeking to know truth and gain accuracy?*
  - To ensure that you are objectively weighing all of the evidence and not just the evidence that you value, ask yourself, *Can I point to clear facts leading to my position?*

Be an Effective Time Manager

When I work with organizations to develop their leaders, I occasionally have the opportunity to interview a leader's subordinates about their leader's mindsets, and they generally identify their leader as being closed-minded. With this information, I then engage in a coaching session with the leader. I generally start by asking the leader about their mindsets. Almost every time, the leader says that they have an open mindset. Upon hearing this, I inform the leader that their subordinates do not agree and ask the leader to explain the disconnect.

A common excuse I hear from leaders is that while they consider themselves to be open-minded, they do not feel like they have the time and space to always be open-minded. Because of pressing deadlines, they must focus on implantation, causing them to unintentionally become closed-minded.

I understand this perspective. During my time at Gallup, at any given moment, I was working on five to ten different client teams, each with a different project leader. What was interesting about this experience is that each project leader largely had the same demands on their plate, but some leaders operated well ahead of deadlines, and others were always being pressed up against the deadlines. This affected the open-mindedness of the project team and, correspondingly, the quality of work that we did.

What I have learned from these experiences is that being open-minded requires intentionally creating the space to do so. If we get caught up in the daily grind, we become reactionary and not very intentional. All too often, we allow our calendar to get away from us and become managed by deadlines, rather than being in control of our deadlines. When this happens, we tend to default to being closed-minded.

This means that we need to intentionally create the time and space for open-mindedness.

Stephen R. Covey, author of *The 7 Habits of Highly Effective People,* says that people can place their attention on things or tasks that vary in terms of importance and urgency. Animating this idea, Covey presented the Time Management Matrix (below), with four quadrants related to the two dimensions. This matrix allows us to investigate how we spend our time and where we dominantly fall in terms of our time management.

	Urgent	Not Urgent
Important	1. Necessity Tasks that need your immediate attention. Reactive firefighting. We need to reduce the tasks in this quadrant.	2. Quality Habitual, proactive actions that reduce quadrant 1. In this quadrant we are able to see the horizon instead of being focused on the immediate present. We need to increase the tasks in this quadrant.
Not Important	3. Deception Things that appear to be worth doing (e.g., email). We can't avoid these tasks, but we do need to manage them, and make sure they do not take away from quadrant 2 tasks.	4. Waste Time-wasting activities (e.g., browsing social media). We need to avoid these tasks

If we spend a lot of time pressed up against deadlines, fighting fires, or only doing things when others need something, it suggests that we primarily operate in quadrant 1. To assess if you operate in quadrant 1, consider: Do you wake up at the last possible moment required of you to meet the demands of someone else, or do you wake up with enough time to invest in yourself and be intentional about your day? Who operates from a position of urgency, and who operates more from a position of importance?

When we operate in quadrant 3, we allow our focus on essential tasks to be hijacked by text messages, emails, or excessive meetings.

Unfortunately, most people operate in quadrants 1 and 3. When we do so, we are more likely to feel out of control, adding fuel to a closed mindset.

If we spend a lot of time mindlessly watching TV, surfing the web, or spending too much time on social media, it suggests that we are operating in quadrant 4. These types of activities are less than intentional.

This leaves us with quadrant 2, the most ideal quadrant for creating the space necessary for becoming more open-minded. Operating in this quadrant provides us with the mental space to sit with new, different, and diverging ideas and the temporal freedom to be able to weigh ideas instead of rushing them and to engage in activities that will enhance our open-mindedness, like meditation.

Ask Others What You Can Do to Be More Open-Minded

If you ask others to give you feedback on the degree to which you have an open versus closed mindset, you can also ask them to give you feedback on how to become more open-minded. This will put yourself into a more open-minded state and will be quite revealing. It will help you better understand the circumstances in which you tend to have more of a closed mindset (i.e., your blind spots) and perhaps why you tend to be closed-minded in those situations. In the process, you will get ideas for quick wins and small changes that you can make to become a better person, employee, and leader. For example, you might receive feedback that you tend to stifle conversation by being the first to give suggestions in a meeting. Chances are, with this feedback, you will be empowered to make minor adjustments that will likely make a major impact. Your renewed ability to seek truth and ask questions will help your team make better decisions. In your family, your enhanced ability to take criticism will help you to become a better spouse, parent, and/or child. Finally, this will help you better understand the impact your less than fully open mindset has been having on those around you, providing the motivation to take the actions and create the space to improve your mindset.

Of this process, Dalio says:

We all have terribly incomplete and/or distorted perspectives...Seeing this will help you evolve. At first most people remain stuck in their own heads, stubbornly clinging to the idea that their views are best and that something is wrong with other people who don't see things their way. But when they repeatedly face the question "How do you know that you're not the wrong one?"...they are forced to confront their own believability and see things through others' eyes as well as their own....Most people initially find this process very uncomfortable. While most appreciate it intellectually, they typically are challenged by it emotionally because it requires them to separate themselves from their ego's attachment to being right and try to see what they have a hard time seeing.

Absorb Information Related to Having an Open Mindset

One of the most helpful activities I have engaged in to enhance my open mindset has been to learn more about the value of having an open mindset, becoming more aware of its positive implications, and recognizing the pitfalls associated with a closed mindset. The following resources have been the most helpful:

- *Creativity, Inc.* by Ed Catmull
- *Principles: Life and Work* by Ray Dalio
- *Deep Change: Discovering the Leader Within* by Robert E. Quinn
- *The Bottom of the Pool* by Andy Andrews
- *The Righteous Mind: Why Good People Are Divided by Politics and Religion* by Jonathan Haidt
- *A New Earth: Awakening to Your Life's Purpose* by Eckhart Tolle

- *The Sin of Certainty: Why God Desires Our Trust More than Our "Correct" Beliefs* by Peter Enns

Summary

To strive for open-mindedness, place an emphasis on seeking truth, develop a healthy fear of not having enough information, cultivate an intense curiosity to learn what stands in the way of your goals, foster an interest for seeing perspectives that differ from your own, and possess a willingness to accept being wrong—and being told so. Let go of your need to be right along with the inclination to give answers, look good, and feel in control.

Altogether, this requires humility, which allows us to create and fuel the culture of psychological safety that is critical for the success and effectiveness of any team: work, family, athletic, and so on. Dalio writes that an open mindset "requires you to replace your attachment to always being right with the joy of learning what's true. Radical open-mindedness allows you to escape from the control of your lower-level you and ensures your upper-level you sees and considers all the good choices and makes the best possible decisions. If you can acquire this ability—and with practice you can—you'll be able to deal with your realities more effectively and radically improve your life."

PART IV

PROMOTION MINDSET

Chapter 13

DISCOVERING A PROMOTION MINDSET

If the road is easy, it's probably easy because it's not a road and you're not on it.

—Craig D. Lounsbrough

The World Cup is arguably the greatest sporting event in the world. The month-long soccer tournament, held every four years like the Olympics, is certainly the most watched sporting event, viewed by an estimated 3 billion people in more than 200 countries. It is contested by the world's best national teams (32 for the men's tournament, and 24 for the women's tournament), who battle for national and global pride and prestige. For those fortunate to play in the World Cup, it becomes the biggest moment of their careers, and with the weight of their country's hopes and aspirations, they face intense pressure.

In case you are not familiar with World Cup soccer, if a game is tied after regulation and a pair of 15-minute overtime periods, then a winner is determined through a shootout. During the shootout, players from each team take turns firing at the goal from a penalty mark only 12 yards away, defended only by the opposing team's goalkeeper. Each team has five chances to score, one per selected kicker. The individual pressure on those shootout kickers is daunting.

Imagine that you are such a player. How would you approach this opportunity, this challenge—especially after playing for up to 120 minutes already and being asked to summon one more strike out of your legs? Do you think, "I have to score in order to help my team win?" Or do you think, "I have to score in order to ensure my team doesn't lose?" Each approach and way of thinking represents a different mindset.

After analyzing all of the shootouts in World Cup history, researchers Geir Jordet and Esther Hartman found that how a player approaches their turn dramatically changes how they behave and ultimately perform. Specifically, they found that when players are faced with a situation where if they miss, their team will lose, they avoided facing and looking at the opposing goalie, took less time to prepare, and converted their shots just 62% of the time. But, when players are faced with a situation where if they make the goal, their team will win, they spent more time facing and looking at the opposing goalie and took almost twice as much time visualizing their shot and positioning themselves. They converted on 92% of their shots.

Promotion and Prevention Mindsets

When individuals approach life and their activities seeking to avoid problems and not lose, they operate with a prevention mindset. But, when they approach life and activities seeking to make gains and win, they are driven by a promotion mindset. These mindsets and their respective implications on our life, work, and leadership rest on a continuum, with prevention on the negative side and promotion on the positive. Just like the prior two sets of mindsets discussed, these have profound implications.

To more fully describe the differences between these mindsets, let's consider how ship captains might operate differently depending upon their mindset.

When captains have a prevention mindset, their lenses are cued in to the dangers of being at sea and they adopt the primary purpose of not sinking. With this purpose, captains become vigilant, seeking safety and stability above all else. As such, they are intensely focused on avoiding problems and limiting risks, as these might "rock the boat" and may jeopardize the safety of the crew.

Being in this mindset, captains are much less concerned about reaching a specific destination or the direction the ship is headed, so long as it stays safe. This means two things. First, without a clear destination in mind, captains have a tendency to take the easiest route possible: following the winds and the currents. Second, since storms only enhance the risk of sinking, the captains actively avoid storms and continually pursue calmer and safer waters.

Captains with a promotion mindset operate very differently. Their primary purpose is to reach a specific destination, and are thus continually focused on making progress toward that destination. These captains don't want to sink, but they understand that storms and treacherous waters may stand in their way. They anticipate such potential problems, prepare accordingly, and become willing to take risks, acknowledging that accomplishing one's purpose—especially something grand—requires taking risk. Thus, the primary goal of promotion-minded captains is attainment, rather than safety and stability.

Both types of captains have the same job, but because of their mindsets, they think and operate completely differently. Effectively, a prevention-minded captain's ship becomes no better than a life raft, blown by the winds and currents, ending up in a destination not of the captain's choosing. On the other hand, a promotion-minded captain becomes willing to brave the winds and currents of the sea to reach a destination of the captain's own proactive design. The prevention-minded captain does what is easiest. The promotion-minded captain does what is best.

Do most people have a clear destination that they are shooting toward, or do they drift, primarily seeking to avoid problems and obstacles? This is the difference between being purpose-focused and comfort-focused. Surely, we know both types of people. But here is the reality: when we do not proactively select a clear purpose or destination for ourselves, our default purpose becomes an approach toward life primarily focused on avoiding problems and enhancing comfort—a recipe for mediocrity.

Which Captain Are You?

A variety of different analogies describe these mindsets. Ask yourself:

- Are you the passenger (prevention) or the driver (promotion) in your life?
- Do you prioritize what is on your schedule (prevention), or do you schedule your priorities (promotion)?
- Are you a product of your environment (prevention) or the creation of your own proactive design (promotion)?
- Do you seek to do what is easy and comfortable (prevention), or do you seek to fulfill a purpose (promotion)?

Between the descriptions, questions, and results of your personal mindset assessment, you should begin to see some clarity on your dominant mindset. Which captain are you? Prevention-minded or promotion-minded?

I have alternated between these two mindsets throughout my life. When I was in high school and heavily involved in sports, I was very promotion-minded. I had clear goals and objectives that I was dedicated to accomplishing, even if it meant sacrificing personal comfort. I made sure that I set aside time every day for some sort of practice or skill development that would get me closer to accomplishing my goals.

After high school, I moved away from home to attend college. One of the things that I quickly learned is that life is not easy. In learning to navigate life, I developed the mentality of "if I can avoid having problems, I will call that a success." That was largely my mentality throughout much of my adult life. I sought to avoid debt like the plague. I sought out a career path as a professor because I thought it would provide stability and a work-life balance that minimized problems. I never considered the idea of being an entrepreneur or starting up my own business, because if I did, the alarm bells would ring in my head: "Risky! Risky! Risky!"

When I took my leave of absence to work at Gallup, it was largely an attempt to improve my risky financial situation, a result of being paid below market rate at a state university, a significant three-year signing bonus about to expire, and living in one of the most expensive areas in the country: Orange County, California.

I possessed this prevention mindset until three things happened simultaneously:

- My position at Gallup didn't work out, taking me back to CSUF.
- During the time between this transition and shortly before a new semester started, I had some time to reflect on where I was in my life. I was not where I thought I would be at my age or anywhere close to where I wanted to go. This motivated me to start thinking more about my purpose and the contributions I wanted to make with my career.
- I dove deeply into mindset research and began learning about the difference between promotion and prevention mindsets.

Between knowing that I needed to improve my financial situation, developing a clearer purpose for my life, and coming to grips with my prevention mindset, I was forced to awaken to my prevention mindset and intentionally chose to put on a promotion mindset. Within a few months of leaving Gallup, and with a developing promotion mindset, I did several things that I never would have done previously: I started my own business, took on debt to hire someone to develop my website with no immediate prospects for generating revenue, and decided to write this book, which included investing in an online writers workshop to learn how succeed as an author.

Looking back on this transition with increased self-awareness, I am now able to see that prior to my shift in mindset, I was rather unwilling to go against the winds and currents of life. When I saw storms on the horizon, I ran to safety, even if my desired destination was on the other side of the storms. I simply lacked the mindset and courage to take on the rough seas and storms that inevitably lie on the path to success. Fortunately, this didn't necessarily leave me in a terrible position, but it did lead far away from where, deep down, I wanted to be and thought I would be.

Since developing a promotion mindset, I feel like I am consistently battling storms, winds, and currents. I am continually pushing myself out of my comfort zone. I am consistently learning how to do new things (e.g., guest blog, get on podcasts, publish and promote a book, land consulting engagements). I throw as many things against the wall as I can, even if risky, so I can learn what sticks and what doesn't to better navigate the seas I am traversing

Let me give you a quick example. When I first started my business, I came across a number of entrepreneurs with similar business models who seemed to be making decent money creating online courses. I decided to try my hand at it by creating a short online course on how to create a standout resume. I invested a decent amount of money and a lot of time to bring it to fruition. Ultimately, I didn't bring in the revenue that I wanted. Rather than consider it a "failure," I saw it as an opportunity to learn what works and what doesn't. I was able to learn that I was not ready to produce and teach online courses. I look back on this experience, and rather than get defeated because it wasn't successful, I now see that by going through this experience, I gained greater clarity on the direction I needed to take and feel that the failure actually helped me speed my progress to my destination.

I used to be scared of the winds, currents, and storms. But after battling these for a period of time, I have learned two lessons: braving the storms isn't as scary as my prevention-minded self thought they would be. In fact, I am finding battling the storms to be fun, and it gives me a sense of the progress I am making.

Why Do People Develop Prevention Mindsets?

Evidence suggests that a prevention mindset might be our default setting. Almost a century of psychological research has repeatedly found that our natural tendency is to choose courses of action that lead to avoiding losses over creating gains and positive experiences. For example, people get more upset about losing $50 than happy about gaining $50. Researcher Randy Larsen has found that negative events and experiences imprint more quickly than positive ones, and we dwell on them longer. This is called the negativity bias, and it suggests two things: our natural tendency is to possess a prevention mindset (our default setting in the absence of a clear purpose or destination), and developing a promotion mindset requires extra inner strength to rise above our default and society's norm to embrace the truth that taking risk is necessary to succeed in business and life.

Speaking of having a clear purpose, I have found that many do not have one. In an informal study I conducted with over 110 participants, I found that while 80 (73%) of the participants indicated that they had a purpose, only 12 (11%) participants who stated they had a purpose were able to articulate it in a way that indicated they had given the matter significant thought. In support of these findings, leadership experts Nick Craig and Scott Snook have found that fewer than 20% of organizational leaders carry a strong sense of their own individual purpose.

When an individual does not have a strong or clear purpose or destination, they generally take on a default purpose of being comfort-focused. They become largely driven to think, make decisions, and behave in ways that maximize their comfort. While this approach is surely justifiable, it leads to individuals doing what is easiest for them, not necessarily what is best.

Additionally, the culture of our environment also shapes our mindset. Organizational cultures vary in their risk aversion, and employees seeking to fit in with their organization's culture tend to adopt the collective mindset of the organization toward risk. Let me give you an example of an organization I recently worked with.

Over the decades, this organization has learned that when a mistake occurs with a client, the client will lose trust and become likely to seek services elsewhere. As a natural response, the culture that has emerged prioritizes preventing mistakes and problems well above adding value and increasing trust. As such, the culture discourages trying new services or approaches with their clients, as they have a greater risk for mistakes and problems. Further, if the organization was going to roll out a new product, it needed to go through an extreme amount of testing to ensure it didn't have any issues or bugs. As a result, the organization was continually late to market with new service tools, resources, and practices. Their prevention-minded culture was leading to stagnation and mediocre service.

The more I work with organizations, the more I realize that this phenomenon is more common than not. Just like people, organizations, if not intentional, are prone to avoid losses more than seek gains, and thus develop a collective prevention mindset. While the leaders of the organization can quickly justify this mindset, they are generally unable to recognize that it unintentionally stifles innovation, creativity, high-quality customer service, and ultimately long-term success.

In all, it is very easy, even natural, to possess a prevention mindset. We tend to tell ourselves that our life is peaceful when we limit problems, we feel safe when we do not take risks, and we are a good team player when we don't rock the boat. But what we have a hard time recognizing is that the absence of problems, risk, and change does not equal success. When we have a prevention mindset, we may avoid failure, but simultaneously we are unlikely to achieve success and greatness.

Are You the Driver of Your Life or the Passenger?

Ultimately, when we prioritize the avoidance of losses over gains, default to a purpose of ease and comfort, and allow the cultures of our environment to shape our mindsets, we become passengers and not the drivers of our lives. This is difficult to see. It was for me. It is easy to interpret movement, busyness, and action as progress. What we fail to see is that those who take the path of least resistance are seeing movement just as much as those climbing the peaks of success, just not in the most optimal direction.

It is only when we identify a destination and purpose and become intentional about our journey that we become the driver of our lives. With this promotion mindset, we chart our own course, become willing to traverse difficult terrain, and resist the downward flow of a current, all to reach the spectacular elevated destination of our proactive choosing.

Chapter 14

HOW PROMOTION MINDSETS DRIVE THINKING, LEARNING, AND BEHAVIOR

Happiness does not come from doing easy work but from the afterglow of satisfaction that comes after the achievement of a difficult task that demanded our best.

—Theodore Isaac Rubin

Martin Seligman is one of the most influential psychologists of our generation. The University of Pennsylvania professor of psychology is the father of a relatively new movement: positive psychology. This movement was initiated in 1998, 30 years into his career, when Seligman served as the president of the American Psychological Association (APA).

A few months after beginning his tenure as president, a small yet pivotal moment occurred for Seligman in a brief interaction with his daughter, Nikki, while he weeded his garden. "I have to confess that even though I write books about children, I'm really not all that good with children. I am goal-oriented and time-urgent and when I'm weeding in the garden, I'm actually trying to get the weeding done," he recalled.

One day when Seligman was in his gardening mode and trying to get his weeding done, Nikki happily threw weeds into the air while singing and dancing around. Seeing his daughter's antics as an obstacle to his goal, Seligman yelled at her. Nikki then walked away for a while. When she returned, the following conversation ensued:

NIKKI: Daddy, I want to talk to you.

SELIGMAN: Yes, Nikki?

NIKKI: Daddy, do you remember before my fifth birthday? From the time I was three to the time I was five, I was a whiner. I whined every day. When I turned five, I decided not to whine anymore. That was the hardest thing I've ever done. And if I can stop whining, you can stop being such a grouch.

Seligman was struck with an epiphany. He realized that raising Nikki was not about correcting whining (Nikki did that herself). Rather, raising Nikki was about "seeing into her soul, amplifying it, nurturing it, helping her lead her life around it to buffer against her weaknesses and the storms of life." He realized that raising children is more than fixing what is wrong with them. It is about identifying and nurturing their strongest qualities and helping them find ways they can best live out their strengths.

From this experience, Seligman resolved to change. Not only did he change personally, but he went on to change the field and study of psychology.

Prior to the turn of the century, an estimated 99% of all psychological research was focused on repairing damage within a disease model of human function and behavior. Very little was focused on studying how people flourish, thrive, and become fulfilled. Essentially all psychology focused on shifting people from negative to neutral states. Very little was focused on moving them to positive states.

Recognizing this, Seligman called upon the APA for increased research on the positive aspects of psychology. A few short years later, he began developing positive psychology, a field of behavioral science focused specifically on the positive aspects of life—what makes it worth living. This catalyzed a change in the focus of psychology to encompass the building of positive qualities.

When compared to traditional psychology, positive psychology speaks directly to the difference between promotion and prevention mindsets. Prevention mindsets limit and fix the bad, largely trying to pull one to a neutral position (traditional psychology). But, avoiding the bad is not the same as creating the good. The absence of illness does not equal wellness. Promotion mindsets, on the other hand, focus on a shift from a neutral or good condition to a great condition (positive psychology).

A relatable example concerns our health. Most people only visit the doctor when something is wrong—they need stitches, to receive medication, or to otherwise fix something. Far fewer visit a doctor purely to improve themselves, take preventative actions, and enhance their wellness.

We can see this mentality in various aspects of our lives. The following table depicts how prevention and promotion mindset individuals view profitability, effectiveness, reliability, ethics, relationships, and coping differently. Correspondingly, these views cause prevention-minded individuals to think, learn, and behave very differently than promotion-minded individuals.

Those with a prevention mindset seek to avoid		Those with a promotion mindset seek to enhance
Being unprofitable	Profitability	Being generous
Being ineffective	Effectiveness	Being excellent
Being inefficient	Reliable	Being flawless
Being unethical	Ethics	Being virtuous
Being conflictual	Relationships	Being caring
Withering	Coping	Flourishing

Thinking

When we do not have a clear purpose, goal, or destination, we develop a prevention mindset and focus on not failing, avoiding problems and risk, seeking comfort, and playing it safe. But when our goals and purposes are clear and activated, we adopt a promotion mindset aimed at succeeding, anticipating problems, taking risks, seeking gains, and making progress, even if uncomfortable. As such, depending upon our mindset, we think about and approach our contexts very differently.

Let me give you a few examples.

As the father of two small children, I'll start with a big part of my daily life: parenting. If I operate without a clear purpose or goal as a parent, I will approach my children with a focus on ensuring everyone is happy and no problems occur. Then, when problems do arise—fighting over a toy, something gets broken, or they take longer to complete a task (e.g., putting on shoes) than I expect—I am quick to get emotional, even angry. My thinking is quickly attuned to solving the problem as quickly and efficiently as possible—not always the most effective approach. But, if I am purposeful and employ a promotion mindset, I become focused on creating positive long-term outcomes, which generally involves helping my children learn and grow. With this mindset, I am not necessarily concerned about whether everyone is happy. I anticipate that problems are going to occur and that my kids' emotions will fluctuate throughout the day. Understanding this, I am able to see problems as opportunities to teach and connect as opposed to fixing the symptom and then distancing myself.

Acknowledging these differences, I see that when I take a prevention mindset toward parenting, I carry a shorter fuse and am much less effective. But when I take a promotion mindset, I am much more level-headed and patient and a much better parent. I see the inevitable challenging moments not as things to avoid but as opportunities to enhance my children's ability to manage their future challenges more successfully and independently.

Second, consider how these two mindsets influence how we think about change. Many believe that people are generally resistant to change. But this can't be correct. We are consistently adapting and doing new things, *if* they are easy to implement and make our lives easier. What separates the promotion-minded from the prevention-minded is the degree to which they value comfort. Without a clear purpose or destination, those with a prevention mindset become creatures of comfort. They see little reason to make difficult changes, even if they would make their lives better. But with a clear purpose or destination, those with a promotion mindset become willing to put off comfort to take on challenges, make progress toward their destination, and accomplish their purpose. For example, losing weight can change one's life for the better. But losing weight in a healthy manner takes great effort, time, and sacrifice. I personally know this. Being in a prevention mindset most of my adult life, I recognized that I could stand to lose some weight, but considering it too difficult, I never really attempted it. My desire for comfort overrode my desire for better health. But, after developing more of a promotion mindset, I decided to make concerted effort to lose weight.

During spring 2018, I was able to lose 30 pounds, and I have kept all but a few pounds off since then. After losing the weight, my body metrics improved (e.g., blood pressure), energy increased, and I feel like I can run forever. I have always been a runner, but historically, I have only logged two or three miles per day. Now, I am regularly running four or five miles per day, with a distance run of over eight miles every weekend. While we might embrace easy change, only those with a promotion mindset will embrace the difficult, yet necessary, change to get from their current position to a more optimal future destination.

Third, consider how these mindsets affect our decision-making. Those with a prevention mindset focus on what can or will likely go wrong, whereas those with a promotion mindset will focus on what can go right. When presented with an opportunity to go on a trip, a prevention-minded person will focus more on how the trip will disrupt their life and finances, while a promotion-minded person will focus more on the wonders and beauty of the experience. Further, when presented with a career opportunity, a prevention-minded person will weigh job stability more heavily than a promotion-minded person, who will likely weigh opportunities for advancement more heavily. Because prevention- and promotion-minded people will attune to different information associated with the options presented, they will weigh their options differently and consequently make different decisions. Sports psychologists Daniel Memmert, Stefanie Hüttermann, and Josef Orliczek have found that those with promotion mindsets produce more original, flexible, and adequate solutions when making decisions.

Since prevention and promotion mindsets shape how we see problems, opportunities for change, and the options life presents to us, they correspondingly shape how we respond to them. The quality of our destination is determined by the mindsets we possess.

Learning

I have approached mindsets with the belief that the pursuit of knowledge and experience is critical to our success. This basic premise is reflected in the following quotes, which you may recognize as long-time fixtures on workstation walls, desktop computer stickies, and water cooler bulletin boards:

> *"If you are not willing to learn, no one can help you. If you are determined to learn, no one can stop you."*
> —**Zig Ziglar**

> *"Continuous learning is the minimum requirement for success in any field."*
> —**Brian Tracy**

> *"The key to success is dedication to life-long learning."*
> —**Stephen R. Covey**

Recognizing a willingness to learn as being critical to our success, ask yourself: Who is going to be more willing to learn, enhance their learning, and become more successful because of it, someone with a prevention mindset or someone with a promotion mindset?

When we possess a prevention mindset, we feel little incentive to learn. Learning generally involves us putting ourselves into the uncomfortable positions that the prevention-minded are subconsciously wired to avoid.

I see this with my college students all the time. Many do not have a clear purpose for their education, other than to earn a bachelor's degree. When it comes time to select their classes, they seek out the courses and professors that they deem the easiest, giving little thought and consideration to which subjects and instructors can best help them learn and prepare for their future careers.

Further, I have observed that my prevention-minded students focus on learning just enough to pass the course. When they study, they generally engage in surface-level study strategies (e.g., note-taking, textbook highlighting, rehearsing), if at all. This differs from my promotion-minded students, who focus on mastering the material and are much more inclined to engage in deep-level study strategies (e.g., creating diagrams, paraphrasing, and using self-testing exercises).

No matter our roles, advancement and improvement require gaining new knowledge, learning new tasks, and developing more skills. It is not unlike climbing stairs. We step up to a new level and adjust to our new surroundings until we are required to step up again. When we have a prevention mindset, we choose to ignore the fact that obstacles and calls for stepping up are coming. We seek to find comfort on our current level and complain or become defeated when stepping up becomes necessary in order for us to move forward. With this mindset, it isn't uncommon for us to attempt to linger on our current plane for as long as possible. But when we have a promotion mindset, we anticipate that a next step is coming and mentally prepare for it, seek to progress on our current level as efficiently and effectively as we can, and welcome the opportunity to step up in order to step forward.

When comparing these two mindsets, it becomes clear which individuals have the steeper trajectory.

Behavior

To demonstrate how these mindsets affect our learning and behavior, let me share an experience I had with my daughter.

A couple of years ago, I took my then five-year-old to try something she'd been asking about for quite some time: ice skating. As you can imagine, when we took to the ice, she was rather unsteady. This I expected. I tried several different things to help her. Always holding her hands, I skated behind her, I skated backward in front of her, and off to her side. An ice-skating coach even came up and suggested we try marching around to get her acclimated to the ice and her skates. So we did. Despite these efforts, my daughter settled on what she preferred—holding on to the wall and scooting around the rink inch by inch. It was very slow going.

After allowing her some time, I started encouraging her to let go of the wall and try moving around without any assistance. Her response? A resounding "No!" delivered with the firm intent possessed by five-year-olds.

As I continued to watch her inch around the arena, I couldn't help but notice other children, some even younger than my daughter, flying around the ice. Some even performed simple tricks and jumps. While I try not to engage in comparisons when it comes to raising and teaching my children, I couldn't help but ask myself, "What leads some children to quickly learn to ice skate and others to not pick it up as quickly?"

As I watched other skaters, I saw one child repeatedly fall, pop back up, and keep going. That's when it hit me: *my daughter was operating with a prevention mindset!* Her focus was intensely dedicated toward not falling. She did not care much about learning to skate, but she sure was cautious about protecting herself. After we were done, she prided herself on only falling once and was unconcerned about the degree to which she learned to skate.

What I learned from watching my daughter and others in the rink is that their mindsets toward ice skating, whether prevention- or promotion-minded, dictate their behaviors and subsequently their speed of learning. My daughter's prevention mindset directed her to seek safety and hug the wall, preventing her from venturing out on her own, which would have enhanced her learning. The children with promotion mindsets were more adventurous, trying new things as a way to develop their skills. Further, I realized that children's ice-skating skill had less to do with their natural abilities and more to do with the degree to which they focused on developing their skills relative to their fear of falling.

This led me to recall my development as a young basketball player. For the first several years, I was definitely not the most skilled player. In fact, I was overshadowed by other, more naturally gifted and athletic kids. But, by the time I was in seventh and eighth grade, I had separated myself from my peers and became one of the best. The primary reason?

I had a promotion mindset. I had a strong purpose to become a great player, which allowed me to focus more on learning and growing my skills than about avoiding problems and discomfort. I was willing to take risks and try out new skills in games, something that my more prevention-minded teammates and opponents were not willing to attempt, usually because they were fearful about looking bad. This included doing layups with my nondominant hand, an important skill to possess. When children first try this, they look very awkward and generally avoid practicing it, let alone trying it during a game. With my purpose to become great, I was one of the first in my peer group to start using my nondominant hand in games. I wanted to learn, even if it meant looking awkward or missing the shot. Most of my peers, on the other hand, were unwilling, largely because they were scared of missing the shot and/or not looking good.

The more I work with individuals and organizations on their mindsets, the more I realize something I have already been alluding to: fear distinguishes prevention mindsets from promotion mindsets. When we are prevention-minded, we have deep subconscious fears that are seeping to the surface. We fear failure, we fear uncertainty, we fear discomfort, and we fear pain. When these subconscious fears define our lives, it could not be easier to justify our prevention mindset. But, if we are able to step back and investigate our fears and related justifications, we are able to see that, while our fear might be understandable in the moment, it is ultimately holding us back. Further, by acknowledging the role these fears play in our prevention mindset, we can create a structure around us to reduce them. In the case of my daughter and her ice skating, we bought her impact shorts and knee pads to reduce her fear of falling. Also, we put her in regular practices to help her learn the fundamentals of ice skating. These efforts allowed her to mentally focus more on her development and less on avoiding falling.

We can all do similarly in our lives. If you have a prevention mindset, what can you do to make falling less painful? What fundamentals do you need to learn?

These are great questions to ask to start your shift from being prevention-minded to being promotion-minded, and simultaneously developing its related attributes: persistence, grit, determination, dedication, passion, courage, bravery, and moxie.

Chapter 15

THE POWER OF PROMOTION MINDSETS TO DRIVE SUCCESS IN LIFE, WORK, AND LEADERSHIP

If one advances confidently in the direction of his dreams, and endeavors to live the life which he has imagined, he will meet with a success unexpected in common hours.

—Henry David Thoreau

Are you a badass? According to Jen Sincero, you are.

Sincero is the author of two wildly successful books about being a badass: *You Are a Badass: How to Stop Doubting Your Greatness and Start Living an Awesome Life* (over 2 million copies sold) and *You Are a Badass at Making Money: Master the Mindset of Wealth*. In these books, Sincero presents ways to help readers improve their mindsets to become wildly successful, while portraying her own personal rags to riches story.

Her story is quite striking. As she articulates in *You Are a Badass at Making Money*, Sincero spent decades of her adult life stuck in "the fetal position of hopelessness and confusion" and "self-righteously insisting that being rich was overrated and gross, and wasn't going to back down easily no matter how broke [she] had to stay in order to prove [her] point." For years, Sincero hobbled along on low-paying jobs (early efforts to be a rock star, freelancing, babysitting, and catering), driving a broken-down and beat-up car, and living in a garage. Within a decade, she was able to transform her life and become a multimillionaire. She now says, "If my broke ass can get rich, you can too."

What changed for Jen? Simply, her mindset. She switched from being prevention-minded, seeking not to lose—or, in her case, maybe not even to win—to being promotion-minded, truly seeking to win. Now she helps others do the same.

What did this transformation look like? While it didn't happen overnight, she had to first push her mindsets forward to become more positive. As this happened, her thinking, learning, and behavior followed; consequently, so did her personal success.

It was a gradual ripening. I do recall one moment when I went to India by myself. I was paralyzed with fear to travel alone, but I had this intuitive hint that I had to do it. It was transformative and beautiful. I also saw poverty and suffering on such a massive scale. I thought I'd be so grateful to go home to my converted shit shack [the garage she was living in]. But when I went home I realized I was so much more powerful than I had ever known and I could do so much better. That's when I started hiring coaches and playing a lot bigger.

Her newfound mindset guided her to take out loans for coaches even before she had the money to pay for them (in one instance, she had to borrow $60,000). She now believed that (1) since winners and top athletes needed coaches to help them succeed, so did she; (2) doing so would force her to work her tail off to pay for the coaching; and (3) achieving greatness and wealth required taking risks. Now she tells everyone, "You have the power within you to create any reality you desire. It just depends whether you're willing to get uncomfortable to create it."

Wasn't that the key lesson learned from my daughter's ice-skating example in the previous chapter?

We all have the power to be successful. Whether we succeed depends on whether we are more concerned about winning—or not failing.

Success in Life

Sincero started on her path from prevention to promotion to success when she realized that, while there was much to be grateful for, she was unimpressed with her lack of progress:

> I felt like I was going through the motions of living my lukewarm life with the occasional flare-ups of awesomeness here and there. And the most painful part was that deep down I KNEW I was a total rock star, that I had the power to give and receive and love with the best of 'em, that I could leap tall buildings in a single bound and could create anything I put my mind to and…only to find myself, a few weeks later, wondering where those few weeks went and how it could possibly be that I was still stuck in my rickety-ass apartment, eating dollar tacos by myself every night.

Those with a prevention mindset are passengers in their lives, usually portraying themselves as victims at the mercy of life's winds and currents. They think their lack of success is not due to themselves but due to the circumstances around them. They react to situations, rather than respond by taking proactive action. Fear-driven and committed to safety, they handcuff themselves to both stability and mediocrity. Unwilling to venture, they become unwilling to gain.

Those with a promotion mindset, on the other hand, are proactive, purpose driven, and committed to growth and success. They are the captains of their lives, dictating their own paths. While the conditions and their circumstances may not be ideal, they recognize that the winds and currents of life are part of the journey and that success comes from how they navigate and respond to the circumstances they face. Rather than settle for stability, mediocrity, and comfort, they are willing to venture out, to push themselves, to perform the difficult tasks to obtain their purpose.

During my visits to organizations to study mindsets, I have gotten to know people who operate with each mindset. Their lives and trajectories are so completely different, it is shocking. To summarize, let me introduce you to a couple of employees: Debra and David.

Debra has worked for over 20 years in largely the same accounting department job. She loves two things about her job: its stability and her ability to leave work at work. While loving these aspects, she doesn't really love her job. She punches the time card, trading her time for money. Throughout her tenure, her primary focus has been to make sure nothing goes wrong, that nothing happens to disrupt her security. While she is dependable, none of her peers consider her a top performer. Additionally, because of her focus on security, she has been adamantly opposed to change. Not surprisingly, I found her and her department using outdated tools, software, and methods. For the reasons above, she did not receive a promotion for 19 years. Only recently did she receive her first promotion, to manager, where she continues to focus on making sure nothing goes wrong instead of advancing the work and processes within her department.

Her home life is not very different. An ardent fan of stability, she sets about on daily routines she is unwilling to change. In the morning, she always has to have her favorite cereal: Honey Bunches of Oats. After, she goes to work, already looking forward to the end of her shift so that she can go home, eat dinner, and put on some TV shows while doing crossword puzzles. On the weekends, her routines include going out to dinner on Friday nights (usually to the same restaurant), running errands on Saturday, and attending church on Sunday. All very predictable.

To summarize, while Debra is satisfied with her largely problem-free life, she is merely drifting. Since she doesn't have a purpose, she focuses on ensuring her comfort and minimizing problems. She is stuck in inertia, doing very little to improve or advance her life. While she doesn't realize it, she is the ultimate passenger, at the mercy of her external environment.

David works in a different but similar organization. He entered the organization as the chief of operations for customer care. Because of his tenacity, collaborative spirit, and dedication to his job and the organization, he was offered the vice president for human resources position, despite virtually no experience with human resources. Those with a prevention mindset would have immediately dismissed such an opportunity, focusing on the problems that could occur. Instead, David focused on the opportunities this position would provide to fulfill his purpose of uplifting the lives of others and accepted the job. His clear purpose drove how he operated in his role, which included setting and accomplishing a goal of meeting all 2,500 full-time employees in the organization within his first year.

David does not see his job as trading time for money, nor does he spend his time outside work in casual comfort. David carries his purpose into his family life. David is intentional about connecting with his wife and children. He looks for and creates opportunities to help his children learn, develop new skills, and experience new things. Fueled by a promotion mindset, David views life as an experience of learning and growing instead of constantly working for perceived ease and comfort. David has put himself in the driver's seat of his life and is willing to brave rough seas to become the person he wants to be and project a positive influence onto others.

It is fascinating to think about the trajectories of each person's life. For the most part, Debra's trajectory has been flat. Things have largely stayed the same for her for 20-plus years, professionally and personally. If asked, Debra would consider this a success, stating something like, "I have had a blessed and successful life, one with great comfort, little stress, and little concern." David, on the other hand, enjoys an upward trajectory, essentially rising to new heights every day. His promotion mindset would never allow him to see a flat trajectory as a "blessed and successful life."

Doesn't it seem clear that what separates David and Debra, go-getters and causal life participants, drivers and passengers, is the difference between having a promotion and prevention mindset?

Success in Work

During the past couple of decades, the amount of research on promotion and prevention mindsets has been so great that a meta-analysis has been conducted. Meta-analyses pull together individual research projects on a given topic and aggregate their findings across the projects into comprehensive statistical summaries. Because they aggregate all of the research to date on a topic, their findings are generally viewed as being conclusive.

The meta-analysis on prevention and promotion mindsets overwhelmingly reveals huge benefits to both employees and organizations if employees possess promotion mindsets. Specifically, it revealed that when compared to employees with a prevention mindset, those with a promotion mindset have significantly higher:

- Job engagement
- Job satisfaction
- Task performance
- Innovative performance
- Organizational citizenship behaviors (behaviors not required of employees, but that help with overall work and team functioning, such as helping a coworker out with a task)

These results not only indicate that promotion-minded employees outperform prevention-minded employees, but they also reveal that the stronger one's prevention mindset, the lower their task performance, organizational citizenship behaviors, and job satisfaction and the more likely they are to engage in counterproductive work behaviors (e.g., gossiping, theft, bullying).

While the results associated with a prevention mindset are definitely not encouraging, the meta-analysis did reveal that there is one benefit to having a prevention mindset: lower safety incident rates.

In all, the research seems to be definitive. Employees or teams with promotion mindsets will outperform employees or teams with prevention mindsets every time.

Success in Leadership

Organizational strategists study why some companies succeed and others do not. One theory they use to explain this difference is upper echelons theory. Its basic premise is that when organizations' top leaders—members of upper echelons—set the strategy and direction for their organizations, they operate through the lens of their personal experiences, values, and goals—essentially, their mindsets. Consequently, this theory suggests that leaders' mindsets dictate their areas of focus, which in turn dictates the direction of the organization. That direction ultimately determines how successful the organization will be.

Understanding this theory and how those with a promotion mindset focus primarily on gaining success while those with a prevention mindset primarily focus on not failing, researchers have investigated whether organizations with promotion-minded CEOs outperform organizations with prevention-minded CEOs.

In one study, a group of researchers from the Swiss Research Institute of Small Business and Entrepreneurship at the University of St. Gallen confirmed that CEOs' mindsets dictate their organization's strategy and direction. Their results revealed that the greater the CEO's promotion mindset, the more the organization excelled in harvesting existing opportunities (called exploitation), searched for new business opportunities (called exploration), and was goal-oriented yet agile (called ambidexterity). Further, the greater the CEO's prevention mindset, the less the organization excelled in exploitation, exploration, and ambidexterity.

In another study, scholars from Oklahoma State University and the University of Georgia found that CEOs' mindsets ultimately dictate the performance of their organization. Their research resulted in three main findings. First, they found that organizations with a promotion-minded CEO outperform those with a prevention-minded CEO. Second, the stronger a CEO's promotion mindset, the higher the organizations' performance, and there was no relationship between the level of a CEO's prevention mindset and organizational performance. Third, when an organization operates in a dynamic environment, the performance gap between organizations with promotion-minded CEOs and prevention-minded CEOs increases.

These findings don't just apply to CEOs. Regardless of where a leader might stand in their organizational hierarchy, leaders with a promotion mindset outperform those with a prevention mindset. Their employees are more engaged, agile, efficient, and creative.

The reason is found in the definition of leadership: the use of power and influence to direct others to goal achievement. This definition suggests that a necessary condition for effectiveness is operating with a central goal or destination toward which the leader directs others. Who is going to have a more inspirational goal or destination, someone with a prevention mindset or a promotion mindset? It isn't very exciting to follow a leader whose goal is to not lose, play it safe, and avoid problems. It is much more invigorating to follow a leader seeking to win and advance to higher levels.

This wasn't always believed to be the case. When research first became available on prevention and promotion mindsets, researchers considered both to be valuable, with their value determined by the specific work context. For example, it was theorized that prevention mindsets would be more beneficial in contexts where mistakes should be avoided, whereas promotion mindsets would work better when innovation and advancement needed to be made.

When I first started conducting research on prevention and promotion mindsets within organizations, I adopted this perspective. In fact, I sought to conduct interviews in departments where mistakes often prove costly (e.g., accounting and payroll) as well as departments where advancement is demanded (e.g., sales, recruitment). Through this research, I arrived at three critical observations related to the role prevention/promotion mindsets play in leadership effectiveness.

First, people can perform any job with either mindset. If a job is intrinsically designed around preventing errors, an employee can perform with either a prevention or a promotion mindset. If a job is intrinsically designed around advancement, an employee can likewise operate with either mindset. The difference is in the approach. Those with a promotion mindset develop a clear goal for how they can push the organization forward within their realm of responsibility. They take a proactive approach to their work. Those with a prevention mindset adopt the default goal of avoiding problems and mistakes. They take a reactive or passive approach. During my interviews with accounting and payroll employees—which place emphasis on preventing and eliminating problems—some employees focused on proactively seeking to develop processes to lower their error rate (promotion mindset). But others just sat back, hoping no errors would occur (prevention mindset). They only kicked into high gear when an issue popped up. Thus, regardless of the primary tasks, leaders can and should encourage a promotion mindset.

Second, in most organizations, a prevention mindset is the norm. Acknowledging that a crucial aspect of a promotion mindset is operating with a clear purpose or destination, when I interviewed managers, the first question I asked was "What is your purpose as a leader and manager?" I asked a similar opening question of the managers' subordinates: "What is your manager's purpose?" I received the same general answer from both parties. Initially, a respondent would stall by saying something along the lines of, "Hmmm, that is a good question," and then rack their brain to try come up with an answer that didn't make is seem obvious that they hadn't given it much thought. The answer that inevitably came out was a rote response, essentially whatever was indicated in the leader's job description. What this indicated to me is that very few managers actually have a clear purpose and destination, which by default means that they take on a prevention mindset.

Third, prevention mindsets are really easy to justify. By nature, people give more psychological weight to bad experiences than good ones. Again, this is called negativity bias. This bias often rears its ugly head in the approach organizations and their employees take toward their customers. Fueled by this strong desire to avoid bad over creating good, organizations and their leaders and employees are inclined to focus on problem prevention in order to retain their customers. In my consulting with service-providing companies, I've observed this to be the approach their leaders emphasize and often incentivize. Leaders justify this approach because they have seen customers leave because of problems. What they fail to realize is that while preventing problems may prevent customers from leaving, such an approach likely does not leave them satisfied, nor will it lead to the positive relationships that ensure retention in the long run. The much better promotion-minded approach involves focusing on adding value in order to satisfy and retain customers. To use an adage from positive psychologist Shawn Achor, "the absence of disease is not health." Again, leaders need to ask themselves, what is more inspiring and engaging: minimizing customer problems or adding value to customers?

I saw this with Alan from Chapter 1. He did not have a clear purpose, so he took on the default prevention-minded purpose: doing what is comfortable, seeking to avoid problems. While completely reasonable to Alan, the approach had some severe negative repercussions. It was uninspiring for Alan's workforce, made worse by Alan's tendency to micromanage to avoid problems. For example, he requested that he be copied on every email communication between an employee and customer. This created a culture where promotional positives like adding value and making a difference were not even on the employees' radars. When evaluations of their services from customers and trainees came in, Alan and his team were more concerned about not getting any 1 or 2 ratings (low performance) than about the percentage of people who rated the trainings as a 5 (top performance). As a result, while customers were not displeased with the services provided, they were not wowed by them either, which led to low levels of customer retention.

It is a night-and-day difference between Alan and David, our promotion-minded human resources leader. David has a clear purpose: to serve the organization's employees by improving their work environment and removing their barriers. This purpose gives meaning and energy to his team because they feel both they and their leader are working to make a difference. Knowing that self-directed employees are much more effective than micromanaged employees, David empowers them with the freedom and autonomy to make a positive impact wherever they see the opportunity to do so. David also is not overly concerned about failure; in fact, he anticipates it. He knows that for his team to achieve their lofty goals, they will need to take risks and be innovative. He is well aware that mistakes and failure are a natural by-product of risk taking and innovation. So, he chooses to celebrate misses because he sees them as a signal that his team is truly trying. Of course, he celebrates the wins too. Because of David's promotion mindset, he is able to create an environment where his employees love coming to work.

Summary

The moral of this chapter is that if you want to be successful in your life, work, and leadership, you need to be the driver rather than the passenger. When you are the passenger, you do not have a clear destination in mind and you allow your external world to determine both your direction and destination. When you are the driver, you control your destiny. You have a clear destination in mind and are taking action to advance toward that destination.

Chapter 16

DEVELOPING A PROMOTION MINDSET

When you are inspired by some great purpose, some extraordinary project, all your thoughts break their bonds: Your mind transcends limitations, your consciousness expands in every direction, and you find yourself in a new, great, and wonderful world. Dormant forces, faculties, and talents become alive and you discover yourself to be a greater person by far than you ever dreamed yourself to be.

—Patanjali

The key to and a necessary condition for developing a promotion mindset and becoming the driver of your life is to possess a clear goal, destination, and purpose.

As I mentioned previously, a time when I had a promotion mindset was when I was in high school. My "destination" was to play basketball at the collegiate level. Fueled by this goal, I built a series of cascading goals, my stepping stones, to provide direction. One higher-level goal I set was to lead my basketball team to a winning season. To do this, I developed lower-level goals that included reading books about leadership and practicing daily, with each workout focused on developing specific skills. I saw myself as the creator of a bright future as a college basketball player.

During my senior year, we started the season strong and were a top-ranked team at the end of the preseason. Then, as we entered season play, we struggled to win. Looking back, there was two contributing factors. First, our head coach had to take a leave of absence because of a family emergency, and our assistant coach did not have the same level of knowledge, skill, and expertise. Second, during the summer prior, my high school jumped up a level in the state's classification system, from 4A to 5A, the designation for the largest high schools in the state. We were actually the smallest 5A school in the state that year. We were competing against great programs that pooled from larger student body populations.

Ultimately, we didn't perform up to my hopes and goals, which prevented me from getting the looks from college scouts I wanted.

The following summer, I continued to chase my goal. I traveled to a variety of junior colleges working out with different basketball teams. I was offered a partial scholarship at an out-of-state college but decided to try walking on at an in-state junior college with one of the best athletic programs in the country.

Tryouts began with the start of the fall semester. More than 60 athletes battled for five spots. I became one of seven people who made it to the final cut. When the list was posted with the names of the five people who made the team, my name wasn't there. I was devastated! Looking back, I don't think I was devastated because I didn't make the team, but because my purpose was yanked out from under me. I felt rudderless and devoid of meaning.

Between losing my purpose and learning that living on my own was not as easy as I thought it would be, I defaulted into a prevention mindset. I thought, "If I can go through college and life with few problems, I would be doing better than most." That became my overarching and prevention-minded purpose for the next 15 years, until I stepped back into academia after my foray at Gallup and began developing a promotion mindset.

In Chapter 13, I stated that my transition from possessing a prevention mindset to a promotion mindset occurred because of three changes in my life: I went through a job transition; I had time to reflect on my life, purpose, and habits; and, with a looser schedule, I was able to dive deeply into learning about mindsets. This got me through the first half of developing more positive mindsets: awakening and coming to terms with the idea that I do not have the most optimal mindset and identifying a better alternative.

However, the second half of the battle required that I move the needle on my mindsets and improve the lenses I use to view the world. I needed to rewire my brain.

Cognitive psychologists have found that the differences between chronic prevention and promotion mindset are associated with asymmetrical activity in our prefrontal cortex. Specifically, when people operate with the right side of their prefrontal cortex more than the left, they are more cued in to the negative and avoiding problems, indicative of a prevention mindset. Conversely, people who operate more with the left side of their prefrontal cortex are more cued in to the positive and seeking gains, indicative of promotion mindset. (This is different from right-brain/left-brain functioning related to one's dominant handedness).

What this suggests is that if we want to go from a prevention to a promotion mindset, we need to rewire our brain to rely more heavily on the left side of our prefrontal cortex. The good news is that our brain is incredibly plastic, making the task possible.

Let me walk you through three actions I took and the tools I used to engage in small repeated practices that quickly helped me shift from a prevention to promotion mindset.

Right after I stepped away from Gallup and reintegrated with CSUF, I took on a role as assistant director for my college's Center for Leadership. In this capacity, I made the rounds with the center's director to meet the center's board members. In one visit, I met Charles Antis, the charismatic and promotion-minded CEO of Antis Roofing and Waterproofing (whom you will meet in Chapter 19). Within minutes, Charles handed me a book that he called one of his "secrets to success": *The Five-Minute Journal*.

While I appeared enthusiastic when he first handed me the book, on the inside, I was thinking, "There is no way I am journaling!" But he went on to describe the book as a tool designed to get into the right frame of mind to conquer your day—and it only takes five minutes. Specifically, the journal includes a morning practice of writing down three things you are grateful for, three things that will make your day great, and a daily affirmation. Then, at night, you write down three amazing things that happened during the day and how you could have made that day even better.

I told myself I would give it two weeks. If it helped, great! If it didn't, no harm done.

I started the daily practices. I immediately realized that by writing down three things that would make my day great, I became much more purposeful. Then, as I reviewed the amazing things that happened each day, I grew competitive with myself to create more amazing things day after day, which in turn made me even more purposeful. Through this practice, I had begun to learn the language of a promotion mindset.

Today, I credit this journal with providing the fuel for my decisions to write this book and start my own business.

As I continued to be inspired to do more and more amazing things, I quickly found that I was having a hard time juggling my responsibilities as a teacher, researcher, entrepreneur, author, husband, father, and volunteer. So, I needed something to help me stay purposeful and directed with everything that I had going on.

This led me to Michael Hyatt's *Full Focus Planner*. The beauty of his planner is that it forces me to connect the dots between my long-term goals and my daily steps. Specifically, on a quarterly basis, it has me set, evaluate, and reevaluate my long-term and annual goals, and it has me set quarterly goals that will draw me closer to these long-term goals. On a weekly basis, I evaluate the progress I made in the prior week and identify big wins, set goals for the upcoming week to move closer to my quarterly goals, and identify my "Big 3" for each day that will allow me to accomplish my goals for the week. It forces me to schedule and prioritize what is most important for accomplishing my goals, and then I can fill in the less important and more urgent tasks involved with my week.

This planner increased my focus on creating amazing days and motivated me to become more clear about my purpose and long-term goals, allowing me to set the destination required for possessing a promotion mindset.

Finally, I decided to give meditation a try. I downloaded the Headspace app and went through their free beginner series. From there, I used apps like Insight

Timer and free meditations on Audible to develop a fairly regular meditation practice.

I didn't see the benefits of meditation as immediately as I had with *The Five-Minute Journal* and the *Full Focus Planner*, but over time, I have come to recognize that the effects of my fairly regular meditation practice resembled what cognitive psychologists were finding.

A team of 10 researchers led by Richard Davidson (from the University of Wisconsin Laboratory for Affective Neuroscience, now called the Center for Healthy Minds) set out to see if meditation can help people rewire their brain and rely more heavily on their left prefrontal cortex (which fuels our positive thoughts and perceptions). They gathered a group of participants and assessed their prefrontal processing. Half of the participants engaged in an eight-week meditation program, while the other half were waitlisted for the program and did not meditate during those same eight weeks. After the eight-week period, researchers remeasured all of the participants' prefrontal processing. Those who had gone through the meditation training were found to rely more upon the left side of their prefrontal cortex when compared to their prior measurement; thus, they were more cued to the positive. Those in the control condition were actually found to rely more upon the right side of their prefrontal cortex, the negative side. These researchers found that meditation literally rewires our brain to be more promotion minded.

I feel like this is the effect my meditation practice has had on me. My almost-daily practice has, over time, helped me rewire my brain to become more promotion minded.

Finding Your Destination

While the daily practices just discussed are critical to rewiring your brain from prevention-minded to promotion-minded, we won't even think about engaging in these practices unless we develop the necessary conditions for a promotion mindset: a destination, goals identifying the steps to get there, and a purpose or "why" that gives us the motivation to brave the winds and storms that may come our way. Yet, identifying our destination, setting our goals, and developing a clear purpose is easier said than done. Performing these actions might be downright foreign and uncomfortable if we operate with a firmly rooted prevention mindset. So, let me provide you with some guidance, direction, and inspiration.

Identifying Our Destination

True success rarely comes about by chance. Instead, we create success by creating it first in our mind and intentionally taking action to bring it into reality. This requires clearly identifying what success means for us, which becomes our destination.

When people, particularly those with a prevention mindset, have not clearly identified a meaningful destination, they adopt a default destination based upon what their peers value. For example, if an individual has not proactively determined a destination to shoot toward, and their friends value nice cars, designer clothes, or a big house, their default destination will likely become the same.

Thus, it is critical that we proactively identify a destination and purpose based upon our own personal values and interests. When we choose a destination and purpose, we are not stuck with that destination and purpose for the rest of our lives. What is of greatest importance is simply having a destination and purpose. As we mature, our destination and purpose will mature along with us.

To start thinking about your destination, here are some questions to consider:

- If you could be anything in 5–10 years, what would you be?
- What does your ideal future look like?
- What are 10 words that you want to describe your future self?

Another question comes from Amy Purdy, a remarkable woman—actress, model, motivational speaker, clothing designer, author, and snowboarding Paralympics multi-medalist. She is a former number-one-ranked female adaptive snowboarder and a runner-up on *Dancing with the Stars* (season 18). She's accomplished now, but she wasn't always this way. In her famous TED Talk, she shares her experience of contracting bacterial meningitis at the age of 19. Doctors gave her a 2% chance of survival, but after losing both of her legs below the knee, her spleen, both kidneys, the hearing in her left ear, and receiving a kidney transplant from her father, here she is. Somehow, she overcame those odds.

Upon being released from the hospital, her life was far from what it is now. Deeply depressed, she wondered, "How was I ever going to live the life full of adventure and stories, as I always wanted?" She went home, crawled into bed, and largely stayed there, seeking to escape from reality. In her words, "I was absolutely physically and emotionally broken."

A single question triggered Purdy's ascendance from depression to accomplishment and put her in a promotion mindset: "If your life were a book and you were the author, how would you want your story to go?" She stopped seeing life for what she didn't have (no legs below the knee) and started viewing new opportunities, such as she could be as tall or as short as she wanted; when she snowboarded, her feet wouldn't get cold; and she could create feet the size of all the shoes on the sales rack.

As you come up with clear answers to the questions above, use a sensory approach to embed them into your mindset. For each answer, allow yourself to go beyond thinking about it and actually try to *sense* it. What does your ideal future look like? What does it feel like? What does it smell like? What does it taste like? What does it sound like? This will help you in the process of committing to your destination, enhancing your promotion mindset, and ultimately reaching it.

Setting Goals

When people want to evaluate whether they have a prevention or promotion mindset, my first question is always "What are your goals?" The clearer their goals are, the more promotion-minded I believe them to be.

I'm a rather conscientious, responsible, and organized person. For the longest time, and because I possessed these traits, I felt like I didn't need to set goals. I felt like I was already on top of things. Now that I am a goal setter, thanks to my *Five-Minute Journal* and *Full Focus Planner*, it is clear that when I didn't have goals, I was a prevention-minded passenger in life, blown about by the winds and currents of the sea I was navigating. With clear goals, I am very much the driver, willing to push and sail forward, no matter what comes along to try to buffet my efforts. While it is not easy, I know that it is the only way to success.

To be the driver of your life, it is essential to set goals. Goals give us power by directing our focus toward relevant behaviors and away from unimportant actions, energizing and increasing persistence, and providing a standard against which we can continually compare our performance, increasing our desire to attain the standard.

Write down your goals. Research conducted by Gail Matthews, a psychology professor at Dominican University in California, found that those who write down their goals have a 42% increase in goal accomplishment. Why is this? First, written goals force you to clarify what you want and to think about, plan, and analyze the steps needed to accomplish the goals and how long it might take. Also, by writing down and reviewing your goals regularly, you will gain insight on the next most important action. Writing down your goals will enhance your intentionality.

Developing a Clear Purpose

Let's go deeper, beyond setting goals, to develop a purpose for your destination. This provides the "why," the motivation to keep you going through the inevitable rough waters, strong winds, and bad weather that you have to traverse on your journey.

In Chapter 13, I noted that in my own informal research, 11% of respondents were able to articulate a purpose in a way that indicated they had given the matter significant thought. Further, it has been found that fewer than 20% of leaders have a strong sense of their own individual purpose.

To demonstrate the importance of identifying a strong purpose, Clayton Christensen, Harvard Business School professor and author of *The Innovator's Dilemma*, shares the following account:

For me, having a clear purpose in my life has been essential. But it was something I had to think long and hard about before I understood it. When I was a Rhodes scholar, I was in a very demanding academic program, trying to cram an extra year's worth of work into my time at Oxford. I decided to spend an hour every night reading, thinking, and praying about why God put me on this earth. That was a very challenging commitment to keep, because every hour I spent doing that, I wasn't studying applied econometrics. I was conflicted about whether I could really afford to take that time away from my studies, but I stuck with it—and ultimately figured out the purpose of my life.

Had I instead spent that hour each day learning the latest techniques for mastering the problems of autocorrelation in regression analysis, I would have badly misspent my life. I apply the tools of econometrics a few times a year, but I apply my knowledge of the purpose of my life every day. It's the single most useful thing I've ever learned. I promise my students that if they take the time to figure out their life purpose, they'll look back on it as the most important thing they discovered at Harvard Business School. If they don't figure it out, they will just sail off without a rudder and get buffeted in the very rough seas of life. Clarity about their purpose will trump knowledge of activity-based costing, balanced scorecards, core competence, disruptive innovation, the four Ps, and the five forces.

To quote Holocaust survivor and psychiatrist Victor Frankl, "Those who have a 'why' to live, can bear with almost any 'how.'"

I have found several resources helpful while developing my own purpose. Several have inspired a significant part of this section:

- *You Are a Badass: How to Stop Doubting Your Greatness and Start Living an Awesome Life* by Jen Sincero
- "From Purpose to Impact," in *Harvard Business Review*, by Nick Craig and Scott Snook
- *How Will You Measure Your Life* by Clayton Christensen, James Allworth, and Karen Dillon
- *Your Best Year Ever* by Michael Hyatt
- *Can't Hurt Me: Master Your Mind and Defy the Odds* by David Goggins
- *The Art of Possibility: Transforming Professional and Personal Life* by Rosamund Stone Zander and Benjamin Zander

- *The Go-Giver: A Little Story about a Powerful Business Idea* by Bob Burg and John David Mann
- *Playing the Matrix: A Program for Living Deliberately and Creating Consciously* by Mike Dooley

Consider some people you know or have seen in the news or in history who have made massive positive impacts on the world. They are sure to include titans of humanity like Abraham Lincoln, Martin Luther King Jr., and Nelson Mandela. What purpose did they have? It certainly wasn't based on safety, security, or what their peers valued. Rather, their individual purposes seemed to be based on making a positive impact in the lives of others. Their purposes were other-focused rather than self-focused.

From my experience working with leaders, the more other-focused their purpose, the more motivated they are and the larger the impact they make. Truly inspirational leaders, individuals others want to follow, operate with an other-focused purpose. It is not very inspirational to be prevention-minded with a default purpose to increase your personal comfort through avoiding problems and losses.

Step into the Driver's Seat

The reality is that you have gotten to where you currently are with your prevailing mindsets. If you're less than impressed with your current situation, it's time to change things up.

In *You Are a Badass*, Jen Sincero says the following:

> You'll probably have to do things you never imagined you'd do because if any of your friends saw you doing it, or spending money on it, you'd never live it down. Or they'd be concerned about you. Or they'd stop being friends with you because now you're all weird and different. You'll have to believe in things you can't see as well as some things that you have full-on proof are impossible. You're gonna have to push past your fears, fail over and over again and make a habit of doing things you're not so comfy doing. You're going to have to let go of old, limiting beliefs

and cling to your decision to create the life you desire like your life depends on it.

Sincero is describing a promotion mindset, being willing to sail against the winds, currents, and storms of life in order to achieve the success of your dreams. The key is clearly identifying your destination, setting goals, and developing a clear purpose

Summing this all up, Robert Quinn, a personal and organizational change expert and leadership professor at the University of Michigan, has written:

> When we have a purpose to which we are truly committed, when we imagine and commit to a desired future, the desired future begins to determine what we do in the present. When we wed a future, we break with convention. We begin to engage in unconventional actions and a new future begins to emerge. When we are purpose driven we are still influenced by our past but we are no longer prisoners. We integrate knowledge with desire and it takes us off the path of least resistance. We move from problem solving to purpose finding. This gives rise to learning and creation.

Rather than being someone who passively waits for success to come to us, we need to create our greater success and drive our lives. Identify a clear destination and engage in promotion-oriented daily practices to develop a promotion mindset and start making progress toward your unique and meaningful destination.

PART V
OUTWARD MINDSET

Chapter 17

DISCOVERING AN OUTWARD MINDSET

Our humanity consists in our ability to sense and respect and respond to the humanity of others.

—C. Terry Warner

D o any of these instances ring a bell?

- When driving, you chose to block someone from merging into your lane, even though they had their blinker on.
- You ignored an email where someone was asking for help or information.
- You withheld gratitude to someone who did something kind for you.
- You failed to do something kind for a family member when it would have been easy for you do to.
- You threw someone under the bus in order to save face to another.

If these sound familiar, welcome to the club! If anyone can relate to these, I can. Yet, I think we have all been there.

When I say "there," what do I mean? It's a question of focus: what was your focus in these circumstances?

You got it?

Our focus in these circumstances was on ourselves. We wore lenses, a mindset, that convinced us that our own needs, wants, and interests were more important than the needs, wants, and interests of those with whom we were interacting. Stated more bluntly, we were seeing ourselves as people of worth and value and others as objects that were less important than ourselves.

In these instances, we possessed an inward mindset. This mindset is on the negative side of the continuum.

It differs greatly from the positive, outward mindset. When we possess an outward mindset, we see others as people and value them as such. We see them as being of equal or even more importance relative to ourselves. It is only with this mindset that we are able to be sensitive to and understanding of others' feelings, needs, and desires and possess a willingness to respond to them in a manner that best addresses them.

Understanding how these two mindsets work and possessing an outward mindset is essential for at least two reasons. First, people in general are very sensitive to whether or not others are seeing them as people or as objects. From the moment we were born, we have been evaluating others' motives toward us. We are well-practiced in gauging others' inward or outward mindset. For example, consider some of your more recent interactions with a significant other, a manager, coworker, salesperson, or grocery checker. Do you feel as though they were seeing you as a person? Or an object? What influence did that have on you? Did it have an impact on your interest in being with or working with them again?

Second, our inward/outward mindset undergirds and influences every interaction we have with others. How we see others and the level of value we assign to them influences how we think and behave in relation to them. When we possess an inward mindset toward someone, it has a negative impact on the interaction or relationship. When we possess an outward mindset, it has a positive impact. This is something that is easy to understand but much harder to practice.

Benjamin Zander

To help these mindsets come alive and to introduce the role these mindsets play in our lives, let me introduce you to Benjamin Zander, the founder and conductor of the Boston Philharmonic Orchestra.

In the music world, a conductor is traditionally seen as a mythical, perhaps somewhat tyrannical leader who towers above the orchestra, dictating to the musicians what to play and how to play it.

Reflecting on his career of over 50 years, Zander recalled that for the first half, he fit the mold of the stereotypical tyrannical leader with an inward mindset. He saw himself as being the most important figure in his orchestras. In his eyes, his musicians were instruments to play the music the way that he wanted it played, rather than people with their own feelings and desires. Zander's primary focus was to gain notoriety, audience appreciation, and critical praise, which would lead to other opportunities and greater success for himself. But that came at a cost: this mindset made it justifiable to berate his musicians, push them to the brink of exhaustion, and limit their voice and personal contribution to the orchestra and presentation of the music.

The result? His musicians felt infantile and submissive. He rarely created space for his musicians to communicate with him, let alone having a role in deciding how to play a particular piece of music. If his musicians made mistakes, he would come down insensibly hard on them. He was willing to push them to burnout not because of what was best for them, but because he thought it was the best for *him*. Zander's mindset created an environment in which the orchestra musicians had a job satisfaction level akin to that of prison guards.

Who do you think is going to play better music: those who feel unsatisfied, worn out, and disengaged, or those who feel cared about, satisfied, and engaged? This is an obvious answer that those with an inward mindset have a hard time converting into practice.

Halfway through his career, Zander had an epiphany: while he was the face of the orchestra, he did not play a note. Even though he was in a position of organizational power and the one who received all the media attention, his true power lay in his ability to make his musicians powerful. Awakening to this led him to develop an outward mindset.

This upgrade and its corresponding results proved dramatic. Zander began to see his musicians as people, even partners in creating great music. He went from asking himself, "How good am I?" to asking himself, "How can I make my players lively and engaged?" He went from trying to gain influence over his players and teaching them his interpretations to being focused on helping his musicians express each phrase as beautifully as they were capable of. He went from not caring about his musicians' opinions to listening to what they had to say. He viewed them as individuals with their own needs, wants, feelings, interests, unique talents, and divine qualities. He began to see his musicians as being as important as, if not more important than, himself.

This led to significant changes in Zander's leadership. At one point during a rehearsal, he incorrectly pointed out that a musician did not come in at the right time. A few minutes later, after recognizing his error, he apologized. After the rehearsal, at least three people came to him and stated that they couldn't remember the last time they had heard a conductor admit his own mistake and apologize. Additionally, he started leaving blank pieces of paper on the stand of every player, inviting them to write down any observation that might guide him to empower their quest to play the music more beautifully. This gave his musicians a voice in what they were creating, a rare opportunity in the hypercompetitive world of orchestral music.

With an inward mindset, Zander's brilliant mind obsessed on the question: "How much greatness can I achieve?" Now, with an outward mindset, his apex question is: "How much greatness am I willing to grant people?"

Can you imagine the difference this change would make if you were one of his musicians?

Take a moment and reflect: How do you see those around you? As people or as objects? Are their needs, wants, feelings, and interests as important as your own?

Getting Real with Inward and Outward Mindsets

Of the four sets of mindsets, the inward/outward continuum can change within us the most rapidly. Literally, in the course of a day, we can fluctuate between the two mindsets multiple times. But, as was demonstrated in Zander's example, we tend to wear a dominant mindset.

Look back on your life and see times when you had more of an inward mindset or when you were more outward. My experience as a teenager, and my observation of most teens, suggests that our adolescent years are largely governed by a dominant inward mindset. We are inclined to think that the world revolves around us. If something does not personally and directly benefit us, we are not inclined to want to be a part of it.

Some people are able to upgrade their mindsets rather easily beyond their teenage years. For others, like myself, this change does not come naturally. Admittedly, this is the set of mindsets that I struggle with the most.

The mindset we wear is shaped by both internal factors and environmental factors. I've always had a deep desire to be seen by others as important and valuable. This has inclined me to place greater emphasis on my needs, wants, feelings, and interests than those of others. Additionally, I was the youngest child with much older siblings, so it was easy to believe that the world revolved around me. I have also realized that in competitive environments, I am inclined to view others as objects as I jockey with them for achievement, notoriety, and positions.

Can you relate?

One of the critical things we need to recognize is that, regardless of our internal factors or environment, we can choose which mindset to adopt and utilize. We can do anything with either an inward or outward mindset. When in a competitive environment, I can allow my natural inward mindset to come out or intentionally choose to wear an outward mindset. As Benjamin Zander demonstrated, we have the power to adjust and change from one to the other, with significant positive effects to our life, work, and leadership.

The key and fundamental thing to remember is that while it can be easy to possess an inward mindset, viewing others as people of value and worth is our most basic obligation. Think of any of the major social movements that have occurred in history. All of them involve individuals seeking to be seen as people of value. If we do not shift our inward mindset, we may devalue others and limit their freedom, contributions, and potential.

Where Is Your Mindset along the Continuum?

Where is your mindset along the inward-outward continuum? More inward? Or outward?

While the personal mindset assessment was designed to help identify your more dominant mindset, we can ask ourselves three questions to assess our current mindset and inspire a more positive, outward mindset. I try to ask myself these questions frequently to ensure that I have more of an outward mindset.

Perhaps the easiest and most simple question is: "Am I being inward or outward?" This quick, powerful litmus test serves to check my current mindset. Sometimes, I will switch it up and ask a related question: "Am I seeing them as a person or an object?"

The next two questions are a little more profound. One comes from University of Houston research professor and five-time *New York Times* number one bestselling author Brené Brown, whose books include *The Gifts of Imperfection*, *Daring Greatly*, *Rising Strong*, *Braving the Wilderness*, and *Dare to Lead*. Her voice is unique and powerful because she has spent her professional life studying a topic that affects everyone in some way: shame.

In *Rising Strong*, she identifies a question that has caused me to see others more fully as people than ever. The question is "Do you think, in general, that people are doing the best that they can?"

What do you think?

There is a powerful backstory associated with how this question came about, which Brown relates in her book.

Upon arriving at the hotel the night before a speaking engagement, Brown learned that she would be sharing a room with another speaker, which she wasn't excited about. When she entered her nonsmoking room, Brown met her roommate, feet up on the couch, eating a messy cinnamon roll. Before shaking Brown's hand, the roommate proceeded to wipe her icing-covered hands on the couch. Shortly thereafter, the roommate went out onto the balcony and began smoking a cigarette. Brown was infuriated because it was a nonsmoking room and she used to smoke.

The following day, Brown met with her therapist, still fuming about her roommate. In their session, Brown vented her feelings, labeling the roommate as a "sewer rat." At the height of venting, her therapist asked her the key question: "Do you think it's possible that your roommate was doing the best she could that weekend?"

Brown responded with a strong no, and then put the question back on the therapist.

"I'm not sure," the therapist said. "I do, however, think that in general people are doing the best they can."

Brown was unwilling to accept that.

Not wanting to let this question rest, she went on to conduct research on the question. As she wrapped up her research, she went out to dinner with a friend. At dinner, Brown asked her the question. Her friend agreed with her and as an example went on to rant about how mothers who don't breastfeed are lazy and quitters. She said, "If quitting really is your best, maybe your best isn't good enough."

This hit Brown like a ton of bricks. Though she desperately wanted to, she was unable to breastfeed her children. In that moment, she wanted to convince her friend that she loved her kids as much as her friend did, and she wanted to tell her friend that she did the best she could.

Brown awakened to how it felt to be seen as someone not doing her best.

Brown then asked her husband the question. After pondering, his response was, "I don't know. I really don't. All I know is that my life is better when I assume people are doing the best they can. It keeps me out of judgment and lets me focus on what is."

Of this, Brown wrote, "His answer felt like truth to me. Not an easy truth, but truth."

It feels like truth to me, too.

Let me share an example I'm not proud of, but it illustrates how this question has changed my life.

For most of my life, when a homeless person has asked for money, I have viewed the request through the lens of an inward mindset. I would see them as not doing their best, which would lead me to want to ask them, "Why are you standing on this street corner asking for money when you can do something more productive with your time, like actually getting a job and working?" When I take this approach to the homeless, I am being quite critical and less likely to be supportive and understanding. And, seeing myself as more important, I justify my lack of support in some form of "I need the money in my pocket more than they do," or worse, "You are not worthy of my support."

But Brené Brown's question started to awaken me to my dominant inward mindset. I was able to see clearly, for the first time, the negative implications of my mindset. This is an essential, although surely uncomfortable, aspect of upgrading our mindsets.

After reading and pondering this question, I started to see homeless people differently, through the lens of an outward mindset. I started to assume that they were doing their best. This led me to ask a question that I had never considered before: "What has happened in your life that has led you to believe that this is the best way to live?" By taking this approach, instead of being critical, I became sympathetic, even empathetic, toward them. I am now much more open and willing to help, because I am now able to understand their feelings, needs, and desires at some small level.

With my historically inward mindset, I have been inclined to assume that others often don't try the best they can. As you can imagine, this has caused me to be quite critical of others and see them in a negative light. Sadly, I'm not alone. When I ask this question to groups, more than 80% state that they do not believe people are trying the best that they can.

Interestingly, through her research on this question, Brené Brown found that those who do not think that people are generally doing the best they can struggle with perfectionism and the resulting shame. Those who think that people are generally doing the best they can are much more compassionate, less judgmental, and healthier in the boundaries they set. Brown found that those who think others are doing their best believe more in the worth of others as well as themselves. In other words, being able to positively answer this question results in us being kinder to others and to ourselves.

The third question is equally as powerful, though perhaps a little more situation based. Think about a time when you were working or dealing with people who weren't as helpful as you would have liked. Perhaps consider group members not pulling their weight on a project, a leader being overly critical or providing less-than-stellar direction, or dealing with unruly children.

In those instances, which question were you more likely to ask yourself: "Why are they not being more helpful?" or "Who am I being that their light is not shining?"

The latter question comes courtesy of Benjamin Zander. He started asking it after he changed from an inward to an outward mindset. When he had an inward mindset, he saw himself as more important and more correct than those he led. When things did not go right, he tended to point a finger at his musicians. But when he developed an outward mindset, he was much more open to the idea that when things were not going well, it was because of how he was leading and communicating, enabling himself to ask, "Who am I being that their light is not shining?"

As a teacher of college students and parent of two children under age 10, this is not always an easy practice for me. However, when a student falls asleep in class (not often) or when I struggle with my children (more often), I try to ask, "Who am I being that their light is not shining?" The question has a profound effect on me every time. It forces me to try to understand what they are seeing and feeling and consider what adjustments I can make to better get on board with them and assist them in the way they need. When I don't frame the question like this, I generally ask, "Why is their light not shining" and become critical. Putting the blame on them means I continue to see myself as doing a great job, when the reality might be that I can do much to improve.

When I ask myself "Who am I being that their light is not shining?" even though I ask the question in my head, my colleagues, students, and children can sense my new outwardness. I can tell it has a profound effect on them, too.

Because our inward/outward mindsets play a foundational role in every interaction we have with others, we must become aware of our current mindset and ensure we either have an outward mindset or are making progress to get there. I hope that by identifying the three questions, you will become more aware of your inward/outward mindset and empowered to improve your thinking, learning, behavior, and correspondingly your success in life, work, and leadership. Here they are again:

- Am I being inward or outward?
- Are people, in general, trying the best they can?
- Who am I being that their light is not shining?

Chapter 18

HOW OUTWARD MINDSETS DRIVE THINKING, LEARNING, AND BEHAVIOR

Seeing another [as a person] tears back the curtain of ordinariness to reveal the astonishing complexity and majesty of each life experience.
—Kimberly White

A s you look back on your life, can you identify key inflection points— actions taken, decisions made, relationships formed, insights gained, or situations encountered—that fundamentally changed the trajectory of your life? Quite often, these pivot points have one thing in common: a change in mindset. For a variety of reasons, they change the lenses we use to see the world, altering or transforming what we see, how we think, and how and why we live.

One of my most profound but also humbling inflection points came the day I learned I possessed an inward mindset. Until then, I carried out my daily life thinking I viewed the world in the best way possible. I had never thought much about my mindsets and was ignorant of my inward mindset. I was deeply concerned about making sure my life played out the way I wanted (a nice way of saying I was self-absorbed), and I mistakenly assumed that everyone regarded themselves and the world around them the same way.

Then, by some good fortune, a book made its way into my hands—*Leadership and Self-Deception* by the Arbinger Institute. Has a book ever been your inflection point? This book focuses on the distinction between inward and outward mindsets and the effect each has on one's life, work, and leadership. It was my first introduction to mindsets.

This book had the effect on my life that I hope this book will have on yours. It awakened me to a deeper part of myself I had never thought about or explored: my mindsets. Reading *Leadership and Self-Deception* was an illuminating, "I was blind, but now I see" experience. What it really illuminated, though, was my inner ugliness. Because I had been ignorant to my inward mindset, I was blind to the effects it was having on how I saw, thought, and lived, and how I interacted with others. As I read, I became crippled with humility and regret. My humility stemmed from being awakened to the reality that how I saw and lived was not even close to the best way. My regret grew from always telling myself that I loved and cared about others. However, I realized that deep within, at my very foundation, the only person I really loved and cared about was myself.

Following this realization, I flashed back to instances throughout my life where my inward mindset led me to behave in ways that benefited myself at the expense of others. It made me wonder how much better my life and relationships would have been had I not been so focused on myself. In my mind's eye, I saw a hill of experiences representing the good I had done and, next to it, a mountain symbolizing the positive difference I could have made—but did not, because of my inward mindset.

I was looking at my mountain of regret.

While this awakening experience was humbling and painful, it was also liberating. I now felt empowered with the knowledge and ability to reset my foundation and mindset to live free of regrets, to live in a way in which I could have the most beneficial effect on those with whom I interacted.

Does this mean I have since lived exclusively with an outward mindset? Absolutely not. I have surely missed opportunities to be a more positive influence on the lives of others because of slipping back into an inward mindset. But, having awakened to these mindsets, I now feel like at least I have a choice on what mindset I wear, and the power is within me to change it. Prior to learning about inward and outward mindsets, I was ignorant of seeing and operating negatively, and I was unmotivated to consider any alternative perspectives. Now, I am no longer the passive passenger to my natural, negative mindsets. Instead, I am the empowered driver, able to navigate my life, relationships, and interactions in the most effective ways possible.

Enough about me. Let's dive into how possessing outward versus inward mindsets drive our thinking, learning, and behavior.

Thinking

The effect of our inward/outward mindsets on our thinking is profound.

Once, I was in a meeting where the topic of parenting was discussed. I was invited to share my thoughts about how we can improve our parenting. I suggested that if we want to become better parents, we must reflect on our pain points and in those moments ask ourselves: "Who am I being that their light is not shining?" I explained how this would put us in an outward mindset and allow us to individualize our parenting to better meet the innate needs of our children.

Immediately after my comments, an individual I have known for several years, whom I'll call Tom, respectfully disagreed with me.

All of my previous interactions with Tom have led me to believe he operates with a strong inward mindset. Perhaps the biggest indicator is his hardline "my way or the highway" approach to how he parents, leads, and manages. This is generally more of an inward-minded approach because it concerns what is easiest or best for the parent, often leaving the parent closed to thinking about what might be best for the child.

In his response, Tom grew emotional, even tearful, as he expressed how sometimes there is nothing more we can do as parents, how sometimes our children go off the "deep end," no matter how good we've been as parent. Tom went on to explain that he had two children two years apart, both in their early 20s, parented in the same way. One became a "model" child, someone any parent would be very proud of. The other dabbled in drugs and the porn industry.

This experience fascinated me because Tom and I thought about parenting in two completely different ways. Tom thought that using the same parenting style with his children was best for all, that he had done all that he could to raise great children, and that he could not have taken any different actions to prevent his daughter's risky decisions. Conversely, I thought that while individualizing one's parenting style to each child may be challenging for the parent, it is best for the children; that we can always learn and do more to raise great children; and that when negative experiences occur, we should choose to reflect on who we are being that has caused their eyes to not shine.

When someone has an inward mindset, like Tom, does it make the person bad? Or even wrong? When I operate with a strong inward mindset, am I bad person? Not necessarily. I didn't go around purposefully doing things that harmed others. Neither had Tom. But, looking back on times I have had an inward mindset, I see how my thinking led me to act in a way that created collateral damage to those around me.

Let me share an example. As I mentioned previously, I grew up playing basketball, with lofty goals of playing in college. Unfortunately, when someone possesses an inward mindset, they generally exercise deficit thinking rather than abundance thinking. Deficit thinkers believe that the rewards of life are a fixed pie, a competition to get as much of the pie as possible. When one practices abundance thinking, they believe that the rewards of life are an expanding pie, and through cooperation, everyone can enhance the size of the pie and get as much as they want or need. With my inward mindset and deficit thinking, I saw my teammates as my competition; I needed to outperform them. This caused me to prioritize playing well and racking up points and rebounds over helping my team win. With this mindset, I felt justified being a "ball hog." At the time, while I could see my noteworthy statistics, I couldn't see that I was negatively affecting my team and teammates. Now, it is crystal-clear. I created a negative atmosphere on my team, and I behaved in ways that limited our collective success.

When we are mired in an inward mindset, we feel self-justified in our thinking and actions. At the same time, we become blind to the largely negative impact our actions have on others. Even now, perhaps after a long day, I will fall back into an inward mindset. When that happens, I am much more apt to get frustrated than be understanding. For example, it is not uncommon for my children to spill a cup or a bowl during a meal. When I have an outward mindset, I view those occasions as teaching opportunities, even an opportunity to bond with my children as we clean up the mess together. When I have an inward mindset, I see those same situations as a huge frustration I have to deal with. Naturally, and unfortunately, I am inclined to get frustrated with and become critical of my children. Because my inward mindset does not want to be inconvenienced, I fail to see the situation as an opportunity to connect with and teach them.

Learning

When we have an inward mindset, we paint ourselves in the very best light. In times of success, we are quick to take credit, usually more abundantly than we deserve. In times of failure, we are quick to place blame on others, often finding it difficult to see how we could possibly be in the wrong. With this perspective, we leave little, if any, room to learn, grow, and develop.

Let's return to Alan from Chapter 1. His management style seems similar to Benjamin Zander's during the first half of his career—seeing subordinates as instruments to do his bidding. He treats his employees as objects and is insensitive to their needs, wants, and interests, asking them to engage in tasks they find degrading and below their pay grade (e.g., clean his personal office). It's no surprise that his organization has experienced a high turnover rate. Blind to his contribution to this issue, and believing he is operating effectively, he has little incentive to change or improve his management.

But if Alan shifted his mindset to be more outward, his ability to learn and improve would strengthen in a couple of different ways. First, how likely is Alan to listen to others if he sees them as objects? What if, instead, he sees them as people of value? He will be much more willing to be open to and value their thoughts, ideas, opinions, suggestions, and feedback. There is a huge difference between our capacity to learn when we believe that others' ideas are as important as our own versus when we believe that our ideas are more important than others'.

Second, consider how Alan might respond differently when problems arise, depending upon his mindset. If entrenched in an inward mindset, he is likely to see problems as being the fault of others, leading him to ask the question: "What is wrong with them?" But, if Alan shifts to an outward mindset, he opens the possibility of seeing problems as potentially his fault, leading him to ask Benjamin Zander's great question: "Who am I being that their light is not shining?" This and similar questions would open Alan to personal development insights that he would be blind to perceiving otherwise. Which of these two options is going to lead to a faster rate of learning and personal growth?

When we operate with outward mindsets, we are able to see ourselves and others more clearly and accurately. This leads us to see the innate value in others as well as our own inadequacies. Both are necessary conditions of humility and its many positive consequences, including enhanced abilities to learn, grow, and develop.

Behavior

Our mindsets create a chain reaction. They first dictate how we think about others, then we behave toward others in a manner aligned with how we think about them. How we see others affects how we behave toward them.

If we see others as objects, we generally end up treating them negatively. Consider a daily activity where it is easy to fall into an inward mindset: driving. Have you ever refused to let someone into your lane, even though they had their blinker on? Have you ever aggressively cut into or around traffic as a way to advance faster than others? Have you ever yelled at someone or made an obscene gesture in their direction? These are all actions that involve you treating others negatively. They are also actions you would take when possessing an inward mindset that viewed the other driver as an object obstructing your path, someone less important than yourself.

When we have an inward mindset, we become willing to justify poor, even unacceptable behavior. There is a great scene in the movie *Hidden Figures* that demonstrates this. During the period where Katherine Johnson is being held back by her colleagues because of her gender and ethnicity, she is seen running across NASA's sprawling Langley Field campus in pouring rain, wearing standard business dress for women in NASA during that time period: a dress and high heels. She is running from the only colored bathroom on the campus to her desk, where she works alongside NASA's lead mathematicians, all of whom are white.

Upon her arrival, Al Harrison asks her, "Where the hell do you go every day… for 40 minutes every day?" In her righteous indignation she powerfully states:

> There's no bathroom for me here…There are no colored bathrooms in this building or any building outside the West Campus, which is half a mile away. Did you know that? I have to walk to Timbuktu just to relieve myself, and I can't use one of the handy bikes. Picture that, Mr. Harrison. My uniform, skirt below my knees, my heels, and a simple string of pearls. Well, I don't own pearls. Lord knows you don't pay coloreds enough to afford pearls! And I work like a dog, day and night, living off of coffee from a pot none of you want to touch! So, excuse me if I have to go to the restroom a few times a day.

What leads to people being treated as second-class or worse citizens? What leads to a roomful of people not stepping in to help when they see another being treated unfairly? At the core, it is an inward mindset, viewing ourselves as being more important than others and others as being objects.

It is only when we see others as people that we engage in what psychiatrists and therapists laud as the most important element of healthy relationships: emotional attunement. Marriage expert John Gottman's blog proclaims that "It is impossible to nurture healthy relational dynamics without practicing attunement." Gottman defines emotional attunement as "the desire and ability to understand and respect [another's] inner world." It is being sensitive to others' feelings and emotions, acknowledging them, and responding appropriately.

Can you think of instances when people did not attune to you? When you were frustrated at work and no one seemed to care? When you had a legitimate complaint about a bill or product and the customer service agent and/or company didn't seem to have interest in assisting you? Or maybe when you felt like your significant other seemed more concerned about the task in which they were engaged (e.g., watching TV) than your distress? How have you felt in these situations?

There is a huge difference between situations where others are unconcerned about your emotions and situations where they attune to you by wanting to understand you, your feelings, and what support you need. Your respect for the individuals who attune to you is huge, while it is generally nonexistent for those unwilling to attune.

You can see this contrast in an experience that Kimberly White writes about in her book, *The Shift: How Seeing People as People Changes Everything*.

Through her work as a consultant for a nursing home system, White grew accustomed to the atmosphere and enjoyed meeting patients. But there was one patient she tried to avoid: Alice. Alice was unique because half of her skull was missing, her head grotesquely caved in over her left eye. Although Alice generally wore a baseball cap, the disfigurement was still noticeable. White sought to avoid Alice because she was afraid that if she looked at her, she might stare in horror.

During lunch one day, White was disrupted because across the dining room, she heard Alice call out to an aide who was walking by. Unfortunately, the aide walked right past her, failing to respond to Alice's call. Without getting a response, Alice muttered the F-word quite audibly.

A few minutes later, the aide came back and Alice called out again, stating the word "Pitcher" in her slurred speech. But again, the aide walked right past her, and Alice reacted with the F-word again.

Then, another staff member came into the dining room, and Alice again called out, "Pitcher!" this time waving her water pitcher. But again, she was passed by without receiving any help, and dropped another F-bomb. Clearly Alice was feeling she wasn't being attuned to.

Now, White felt like she was in a bind. Should she attune to Alice, anticipating the awkwardness that might result? Or continue to eat her lunch in peace? In deciding what to do, White flashed back to memories when she had experienced her own head injury and the resulting trouble producing the names of common household objects. In those instances, while she knew what she wanted to say, her brain, at times, wouldn't access the words for the objects, a condition called aphasia. She remembered how frustrating and embarrassing that was.

She saw that same frustration and embarrassment on Alice's face.

Before she knew it, White was on her feet walking over to Alice. Helping Alice get some water, White empathized with the frustration of not being able to get the right sounds and words out. She then spent some time getting to know Alice and making sure she got what she wanted.

White writes that she has a hard time putting to words the feelings that came over her in that moment. She'd been talking to Alice for several minutes without much thought to Alice's misshapen head, something she feared before. While just inches away, instead of seeing her disfigurement, White saw her as a person.

After they finished, White wanted to "run, jump, and dance around." She felt so excited inside that she wanted to express it outside. She felt that the day she was living mattered to someone else. White continues, "I couldn't remember the last time someone else's life was better because of me.

Before this experience, White looked at Alice through an inward mindset lens. This caused her to be absorbed in her own self and concerns—she doesn't feel comfortable looking at misshapen heads. Only after White put on an outward mindset was she able to see Alice as a person with needs and wants, and step in to help.

As I write this story, my eyes tear up because I can feel the power of this moment, the power an outward mindset and subsequent attunement can make. I also tear up because I am forced to admit that far too often I pass up opportunities to make others' lives brighter and better because of my inward mindset.

Summary

A core message of this book has been that how we see our situations and the people we associate with changes how we think about them. It is only when we have an outward mindset that we are able to see and appreciate the true value of others. Having an outward mindset is the only way to see and appreciate the true value of ourselves relative to others.

Let me summarize this chapter by identifying five ways our inward/outward mindsets cause us to see ourselves and others in different ways. As you read each, consider: "Which perspective is the 'truer' perspective?"

	Inward	Outward

How we view ourselves	We are more important than others, and the world revolves around us	We think about ourselves as one piece of a larger puzzle, with all of the pieces playing an important role in the grand masterpiece called life
	Inward	**Outward**
How we view others	Others are objects or resources there to help us or at least stay out of our way	Others are people and partners of great value
How we view others' feelings, needs, and emotions	We dehumanize others and do not consider their perspective or their feelings, needs, or emotions	We humanize others, which leads us to seek out their perspective and consider their feelings, needs, and emotions
How we view others' thinking, actions, and efforts	We think that others are not trying their best, often leaving us judgmental and critical of them	We think that others are trying their best, which leads us closer to empathy and away from judgment and criticism
How we view failure and negative experiences	Negative experiences are the fault of others	We at least question the role that we played in the failure or negative experience

In all, when we have an outward mindset, we see more clearly, become much more grounded in reality, and become much more in tune with those around us.

Chapter 19

THE POWER OF OUTWARD MINDSETS TO DRIVE SUCCESS IN LIFE, WORK, AND LEADERSHIP

To add value to others, one must first value others.
—**John C. Maxwell**

Michael Arndt achieved the pinnacle of success in screenwriting. He wrote the screenplay for *Little Miss Sunshine*, which won Academy Awards for both Best Picture and Best Original Screenplay. He also wrote the screenplays for *Toy Story 3*, *The Hunger Games: Catching Fire*, and *Star Wars: The Force Awakens*.

Michael has learned a secret that filmmakers must know for a film to be successful. He says that at some point, filmmakers must pivot from creating the movie for themselves to creating it for others. It is the slightest change in perspective, one from an inward mindset to an outward mindset, but if it does not happen, it can doom the film.

While this shift is essential for success, it also can be painful. "Part of the suffering involves giving up control," he says, meaning that filmmakers need to let go of things they might personally love or value but are not working. He continues, "I can think it's the funniest joke in the world, but if nobody in that room laughs, I have to take it out. It hurts that they can see something you can't."

All too often, what stands between us and our greater success is the unwillingness to do what Michael suggests: let go of what we want and pivot toward what is best for those we are serving. When we have an inward mindset and are consumed with our personal importance, it makes pivoting and letting go all the more difficult.

In this chapter, we will explore what possibilities lie in store for us if we can develop a more outward mindset and loosen our grip on who we think we are and what we think is best.

Success in Life

Imagine how the first few hours of your day might go wearing an inward mindset. After getting out of bed, you walk into the kitchen and find the sink full of dishes. You immediately become judgmental and critical of your spouse, significant other, or roommate, because the sink full of dishes is tangible evidence that they are not trying their best, and that they are unconcerned about the inconvenience of leaving you to do the dishes. Next, you step to your computer and punch away at an email. Just as you're getting engrossed in it, a child, spouse, or roommate interrupts by shoving a toy at you for play or insisting you read a social media post that is not as interesting as they think it is. You (politely) explain that you are in the middle of something and get right back to it—failing to recognize the light in their eyes dimming a little.

Then, as you head off to work, stuck in traffic resembling a full parking lot, you look in the rearview mirror and see a car driving along the shoulder for a while, attempting to bypass dozens of cars, and then the driver tries to cut you off in order to get back into an appropriate lane. Reluctantly, you let them in, but in the process, you let them know of your displeasure by laying on the horn and flipping the bird.

All of this happens before you even arrive at work. Now imagine how your day might proceed if you continue in this mindset.

How much of this, or something akin to it, resembles your life? Does living in this way reflect what you would consider to be a successful life? Or does a successful life look and feel more like being more empathetic to others' situations, seeing small interactions as opportunities to make others' eyes shine, and letting the little things roll off our backs while we give others the benefit of the doubt?

While our inward/outward mindset affects many aspects of our lives, it especially impacts our relationships. Those with an inward mindset often undervalue the role high-quality relationships play in their lives. They are inclined to view relationships as short-term, feel-good companionships that exist to benefit them in the moment. Those with an outward mindset see high-quality relationships as central to a happy and fulfilling life.

If positive and enduring relationships are an important part of how you define a successful life, and there is any part of you that wants to improve your relationship with a spouse, children, parents, siblings, friends, or colleagues, it is necessary to develop an outward mindset or improve upon your current mindset.

To demonstrate, consider these questions:

1. Can you tell when someone views you as an object?
2. How does it feel when someone views you as an object?
3. How interested are you in building a relationship with someone who views you as an object?

How did you answer these? Were you able to provide straightforward answers?

The implications of this assessment are significant. Not only can we tell how other people feel about us, but we respond to their feelings toward us much more than their actual behaviors. For example, has anyone done something nice for you but only because they wanted a favor in return? A little quid pro quo? How did you respond? How was that different from a situation in which someone acts in kindness or goes out of their way because they genuinely care about you as a person?

Flipping this thinking around, other people can tell how you feel about them, and they respond to you accordingly. If they sense that you see them as being of value, they will treat you with value. If they sense you see them as an object, they will treat you as an object. If you want better and more fulfilling relationships in your life, it is essential to enhance your outward mindset and improve the degree to which you see the value in others.

Success in Work

When I ask business professionals how important trust is in organizations, on a scale of 1 to 10, with 10 being "very important," I rarely get people who respond with an answer less than a 9. We seem to recognize that trust is critical for our own professional success as well as the success of our teams and organizations.

Yet, when I ask these professionals what the level of trust is within their organizations, the majority respond by indicating a level below 7. Research confirms their responses. Various long-standing sources, including *Forbes*, *Fast Company*, and *Industry Week*, have reported the following statistics:

- 82% of employees don't trust their boss to tell the truth.
- Only 24% of employees believe their CEO exhibits ethical behaviors.
- Only 49% of employees say they trust their senior managers.
- Only 36% of employees believe their leaders act with honesty and integrity.
- Over the past 12 months, 76% of employees have observed illegal or unethical conduct on the job, which, if exposed, would seriously violate public trust.

If we are to believe these statistics, trust seems like something we only give lip service to. We say it is important, but when push comes to shove, leaders, managers, and employees feel comfortable damaging trust for the sake of productivity and profitability. We fail to recognize that there is a solid economic case for trust. In Stephen M. R. Covey's book *Speed of Trust*, he reveals that as trust goes up, speed of performance and productivity rises while costs fall. As trust goes down, speed goes down and costs go up.

What is at the root of so much distrust within organizations? I contend that its heart is an inward mindset driven by fear. When individuals are fearful of being passed up, evaluated poorly, or scrutinized in any fashion, they are naturally going to turn inward to self-protect. When they turn inward, what is likely to happen to trust and the quality of relationships in the workplace? Speed will go down, and costs will go up.

If we want the trust and quality relationships that lead to employee and organizational success, we must develop and maintain an outward mindset and create a culture that sees others as people of value.

In Chapter 11, I mentioned some analyses I did at Gallup, exploring which of 12 particular qualities seemed to be the most important for engagement. I identified "My opinions count at work" as being the most important for ensuring employees are engaged at work. The second most important item is one that requires an outward mindset: "Someone at work cares about me as a person." Across nine organizations and almost 60,000 employees, I found that 42% of employees cannot "strongly agree" that someone at work cares about them as a person. When employees felt this way, I found that only 12% of them were engaged in their work. The message is simple: if employees are not viewed and valued as people, they are not likely to be engaged in their work.

This is what Benjamin Zander found. During the first half of his career, when he was primarily focused on and concerned with making a name for himself, he was simultaneously fearful of criticism—a perfect recipe for an inward mindset. Caring more about his success than the feelings of his musicians, he treated them as instruments to his fame and fortune, which resulted in his musicians experiencing low satisfaction, trust, and engagement.

Do you think that this made Zander's job of leading and motivating his musicians easier or more difficult? Do you think this increased Zander's odds of achieving success or limited them?

Zander's emphasis on his success caused him to lead in a manner that was not only making his job more challenging but preventing his musicians from playing at their best. Ironically, his search for success was ultimately limiting the success he was seeking. It was only after Zander was able to look past himself, put on an outward mindset, and value his musicians as people that he was able to create a working environment that brought out the best in his musicians and led to greater success for the orchestra.

The lesson here is compelling. The more we focus on our own success, the harder our road to get there. The more we focus on the feelings, needs, and success of those we rely upon for our success, the easier our road to get there. But this lesson extends beyond personal success to team and organizational success. Consider two examples.

Remember Charles Antis, the CEO of Antis Roofing and Waterproofing, who gave me my first *Five-Minute Journal?* Prior to that first meeting, the director for the Center for Leadership and I had met other board members. They generally had similar titles, but at much larger organizations, primarily in the corporate sector, not the roofing industry. Against that backdrop, I have to admit, I was a little skeptical about meeting Antis. I ignorantly wondered what voice he could lend to leadership.

The instant I met Antis, I understood. He is a charismatic leader with a purpose of giving to better the community. He has been a generous giver for years, donating the roofs for all Habitat for Humanity homes constructed in Orange County, California. But a few years ago, he stepped it up a notch. His extreme outward mindset led him to set a personal goal of saying yes to anyone who asked for his support or help. Since setting that goal, not only has his giving skyrocketed, but simultaneously so has his business, his influence in the community, and the awards he and his business receive on a local and national basis. In fact, Antis Roofing and Waterproofing was recently awarded the US Chamber of Commerce Foundation Corporate Citizen Award.

Antis realizes that the secret to success is not about trying to become successful. Rather, it is about trying to *help others* become successful. The result of this outward mindset-fueled perspective has profound implications for both business and community. Internally, Antis's employees have a clear purpose beyond fixing roofs. Fixing roofs not only keeps their customers safe and dry, but it provides the means to have a positive impact on the broader community. Driven by purpose, employees stick with the company, turning over at a small fraction of the rate compared to the broader roofing industry. Externally, they strengthen the community by supporting Ronald McDonald House Charities, nonprofit leadership programs, and taking a lead in Orange County's homelessness problems.

Let's head 1,500 miles east of Orange County to consider a similar jaw-dropping impact, this created by the Kansas City SWAT team. For years, Kansas

City police viewed criminals through an inward prism, as objects worthy of arrest and incarceration. With this mindset, it was not uncommon for them to use excessive force, spit tobacco on suspects' furniture, or put bullets into potentially dangerous dogs. This led to SWAT receiving the most complaints within the Kansas City Police Department, on average two to three per month, costing the department an average of $70,000 per incident in legal fees and damages.

Supervisors recognized that something needed to change. They brought in the Arbinger Institute, a consulting group whose focus is helping organizations upgrade their inward/outward mindsets. The effects were substantial and immediate. Initially, the thinking and behaviors of SWAT team members changed. They started to see criminals as people and thus treated them with greater respect. They stopped chewing tobacco on raids. They brought in a dog specialist to teach them how to better control potentially dangerous animals without shooting them.

The results were profound. The SWAT team progressed from enduring two or three complaints per month to not receiving a single complaint *for over six years*. Since they were treating people with greater respect, those citizens were more willing to cooperate with them, leading them to recover more drugs and guns in the next three years than they had the previous decade.

What do you think it is like to work at Antis or with the Kansas City SWAT team? Do you think the employees are proud of the impact they are making on their communities? Do you think the potential for greater impact through their jobs excites them? Do you think they are operating in a way that leads to being recognized, promoted, and getting raises?

The answer to these questions is a resounding yes.

We all want to be successful in our work. We want to be recognized, be promoted, and meaningfully contribute to the profitability of the organization we work for or run. Within our desires and attempts, what do we focus on? Most of us naturally focus on things associated with having an inward focus: being seen, playing the political game to get on high-profile projects, and driving the numbers that make us look good. This causes us to overlook the fact that an outward mindset is a key driver of professional and organizational success.

When we have an outward mindset, we think, learn, and behave in ways that naturally bring about success. Rather than teams experiencing in-fighting and jockeying for positions and resources, there is out-helping. As demonstrated through the examples of Benjamin Zander, Antis Roofing and Waterproofing, and Kansas City SWAT, such an approach leads to greater success.

Success in Leadership

In Chapter 15, I defined leadership as the use of power and influence to direct others to goal achievement. This definition implies two things:

- One does not need to be in a formal leadership position to be a leader, and, conversely, a person in a formal leadership position may not be a leader if incapable of directing others to goal achievement.
- The foundational ingredients of leadership are power and influence.

For a moment, identify three people who hold power and influence over you. What allows them to have this influence?

While many have the ability to influence us, the reasons for this can differ. For example, your spouse likely influences you and how you operate. But why do they have this power and influence? Because you admire and respect them for the love they have demonstrated to you? Or perhaps because they can withhold things you desire, such as sex or money to buy a coveted item? Additionally, your manager likely has power and influence over you. But again, the reasons for this power and influence can differ. For one person, their manager may essentially control the quality of their work environment and career trajectory, but for another, their manager could be someone they greatly respect.

The difference in why and how people hold power and influence over us boils down to the power base they choose to lead with. There are two primary power bases leaders can rely upon: organizational and personal. When one leads from an organizational power base, they rely upon their position of authority to wield rewards or punishments as ways to entice or coerce movement toward a desired goal. People follow because they feel like they *have* to. When one leads from a personal power base, they view their power as derived from respect and seek to influence others not through rewards or punishments but because of the value they can provide and the qualities they possess. People follow those with personal power because they are worthy of being followed, and thus they *want* to follow them.

Which of these two power bases is most commonly used in a corporate setting? From my experience working with organizational leaders, most rely upon organizational power. Why? Because it is easier to gain and wield. Essentially all one has to do to gain such power is be placed in a position of authority. Once in that position, in order to influence and motivate others, they only need to offer up rewards or threaten with punishments. This approach to leadership is going the easy route. It requires nothing of the leader other than advancing into a position of power. Personal power, on the other hand, is more difficult to gain and wield. It requires something of us: becoming someone others want to follow, which takes time and investment in personal development and relationships.

Now for the more important question: Which power base is more effective to lead from? Surely, organizational power can get the job done, particularly in the short-term. But it usually has significant and long-term negative side effects. As an extreme example, think of 20th century German chancellor and megalomaniac Adolf Hitler and his regime. Or, as a business example, think of "Chainsaw" Al Dunlap. According to *Time* magazine, he is considered one of the "Top 10 Worst Bosses" of all time. He gained this notorious title because his approach to generating profits for organizations was to "cut down" or lay off employees. Commenting on Dunlap, journalist John A. Byrne, the author of Dunlap's biography, wrote:

> In all my years of reporting, I had never come across an executive as manipulative, ruthless, and destructive as Al Dunlap...[He] sucked the very life and soul out of companies and people. He stole dignity, purpose, and sense of organizations and replaced those ideals with fear and intimidation.

These people had a huge amount of power and influence and accomplished much, largely through authority and coercion, but at what cost?

When I read statistics related to the effectiveness of leaders and managers, it seems clear to me that most managers lead from an organizational power base. These statistics include:

- 3 in 5 employees would prefer to have a different boss compared to higher pay.
- 1 in 3 employees report a "somewhat positive" or worse relationships with their manager.
- 3 in 5 employees report that their manager damages their self-esteem.
- 2 in 5 employees report that their manager does not help them be more productive.

The more effective way to lead is from a personal power base. This requires us to become someone worthy of followership because of the person we are, not the position we hold. As we become such a person, we gain a healthy influence on others. We create an environment where people *want* to work, rather than feel like they *have* to work. Operating in this way provides us the opportunity to leave a positive, influential, and even life-changing mark on the lives of those we lead. Rarely are the following comments made about someone who leads with organizational power:

- She was the best manager and leader I have ever worked with.
- He helped me to become the person I am today.
- She wasn't just my manager; she was my mentor and helped me get my big break.
- Because of what he has done for me, I would jump into a burning house for that man.

It is critical to understand the role our inward or outward mindsets play in the power base we primarily rely upon.

When we have an inward mindset, our thinking is cued into doing what is easiest and most convenient for ourselves. We lead in a way that leverages our authority and brings quick returns on our efforts, which means relying primarily upon rewards and punishments to get people to do what we want. Rather than investing in building relationships with those we lead, we consider them objects and pawns to fulfill our needs and interests, often regardless of the costs to them. While we may compel them into working the weekend to help meet our goals or deadlines, we in turn show little regard for the negative impact the extra work— or lack of days off—might have on them.

When we lead in such a way, there is very little reason for employees, colleagues, or team members to want to follow and be influenced by us. If they feel like an object, how are they likely to see us? Probably as objects, too.

When we treat others as objects, are they going to work at their best, smartest, hardest, and most skilled level? No. They will hover right above the red line of mediocrity and reprimand, often forcing the leader into relying more and more upon his or her authority and the use of rewards and punishments to get work done. It becomes a vicious cycle of frustration, with the leader becoming increasingly agitated with their employees' relative ineffectiveness, and workers growing increasingly dissatisfied by being seen and treated like objects.

Conversely, when we have an outward mindset, our thinking is cued into doing what is best for those we lead. Rather than leveraging our authority and relying upon the use of rewards and punishments, we try to develop the characteristics of a leader that others want to follow and set an example. Additionally, we recognize that our ability to influence others is contingent upon the quality of our relationship with them. This leads us to invest in and develop meaningful relationships with those we lead.

David, the newly promoted head of human resources for a large organization we met in Chapter 15, told me of an interaction he recently had with one of his subordinates, Alex, who had been with the organization for 30 years. In the meeting, David asked Alex about his goals for the rest of his career. "I don't know; I have never been asked that before," Alex replied.

From this simple surprising answer, what can you imply about Alex's prior leaders and the power base they led from? How willing do you think Alex is to follow and be influenced by David? I'd say pretty likely. In fact, David is the type of leader for whom employees would run into a burning building. He has been manifesting his outward mindset by setting and fulfilling his goal of personally meeting all 2,500 full-time employees in the organization in his first full year in his position.

Hopefully, you are getting a sense of how a leader adopting an outward mindset can influence the entire culture of a workgroup. If you are viewed as not only a person but a valuable partner, a stakeholder in whatever the task is, you are likely to work at your best, smartest, hardest, and most skilled level. To quote the Arbinger Institute in *Leadership and Self-Deception*, we "don't know how much smarter smart people are, how much more skilled skilled people get, and how much harder hardworking people work when they see, and are seen, straightforwardly—as people."

Rather than creating a vicious cycle of frustration, leading from a personal power base creates a virtuous cycle of empowerment. Outward leaders entrust their followers with responsibilities. As the workers excel in their roles, driven by their desire to follow their leader, they enhance the trust their leader holds in them. In turn, this leads to greater responsibilities and empowerment.

Your effectiveness as a leader is grounded in the degree to which you have an outward mindset. Having an outward mindset:

- Leads those around to you to have an outward mindset.
- Fuels the effort, skills, and intelligence of those you lead.
- Creates a virtuous cycle of empowerment, as opposed to a vicious cycle of frustration.

This holds across all contexts in which we might be a leader: an organization, family, the military, church, you name it.

These effects can be seen in research that I have conducted on these two mindsets. Working with an organization with about 2,000 employees, I was able to survey employees on the degree to which they felt their leader had an inward/outward mindset. Then, four weeks later, I asked those same employees about their perceptions of their work environment. What I found is that if employees rated their leader in the bottom quartile, indicating a strong inward mindset, they rated their trust in their leader, sense of inclusiveness, and sense of psychological safety at 3.29, 3.94, and 3.92, respectively, on a 1–7 scale ranging from strongly disagree to strongly agree. Essentially, one quarter of all employees felt strongly that their leader saw them as an object and could not agree that they trusted their leader, felt included, or felt safe in their role. One quarter! But, if employees rated their leader in the top quartile, indicating a strong outward mindset, they rated their trust in their leader, sense of inclusiveness, and sense of psychological safety at 6.59, 5.86, and 5.60, respectively. For trust, that is more than a 100% increase.

Summary

In *Leadership and Self-Deception*, the Arbinger Institute, referring to the importance and consequences of inward/outward mindsets, states: "The thing that divides fathers from sons, husbands from wives, neighbors from neighbors [is] the same thing [that] divides coworkers from coworkers as well. Companies fail for the same reason families do." Inward mindsets.

Ultimately, as human beings, our most basic responsibility is to see others as people of value. This requires an outward mindset. If we can upgrade our mindsets to be more outward, we will enhance the quality of our relationships, improve our effectiveness at work, and become leaders others want to follow and be influenced by.

Chapter 20

DEVELOPING AN OUTWARD MINDSET

We're all human, aren't we? Every human life is worth the same, and worth saving.

—J. K. Rowling

Look back on your life and identify your most meaningful experiences. In those moments, did you have an inward or outward mindset?

My most meaningful experiences came when I was able to shift into an outward mindset. Allow me to share two personal meaningful experiences: my first taste of having an outward mindset and a minor instance that had a profound effect on me.

Guatemala

When I was 13, my parents and I did something for Christmas that I was not particularly happy about, although I was excited for the adventure. Rather than give and receive presents, my parents and I joined a humanitarian group to help out a small village in Guatemala.

Our group comprised over 30 people. Half of our group was dentists and dental hygienists who would be providing dental care, largely pulling teeth. The other half was tasked with helping to install a new water system. This was the group that I was a part of, led by my dad, a civil engineer. We would be finding an uncontaminated spring, damming it up, and then laying pipe from the spring to a concrete reservoir built by a previous humanitarian expedition. My job would be machete duty. I would be spending much of the week hacking a clear path for all the workers and pipe.

We flew out Christmas morning and, after a rerouted flight, landed in the thick humidity of Guatemala. For the next 10 days, we would be camping in a schoolhouse in a small village tucked in the lush jungle mountains. To get there, we had a 10-hour winding bus ride and a long hike.

Nothing in my middle-class Utah upbringing had prepared me for the poverty and desperation I would encounter.

At the center of the small village, nestled in the valley of the surrounding hillsides, sat the schoolhouse, our lodge. It stood on the edge of the main dirt road, now muddy. Despite it being the dry season, it misted almost the whole time we were there. The road did triple duty as a thoroughfare, soccer field, and roaming ground for pigs and dogs.

As I scanned the hillsides, I could see small lean-to houses peeking out of the trees. I also saw that the hillsides were covered in a lush green bush about the height of a man: coffee plants. All of the families in the area picked coffee for a living, making $10 per ton. After picking the beans, the men and boys had to haul their coffee down the muddy and slippery hillside with 30- to 60-pound sacks on their backs.

Continuing to take in my surroundings, I noticed a piece of bamboo, sliced in half lengthwise, protruding from the bushes on the opposite side of the road. A small trickle of water dribbled from it. This was the village's source of water for drinking, bathing, and washing clothes. I later found out that it was contaminated and a primary cause of disease among their children—which, in turn, led to a high child mortality rate.

As a middle-class kid from Utah, I was floored, wondering how in the world people could live like this.

For the next nine days, my group hiked several miles through the wet and muddy hillside to a spring. We cleared it out, dammed it up, and started laying pipe. At the end of each day, we returned to the schoolhouse to help the dentists, who had a never-ending stream of people waiting to see them. People came from miles away, many walking through the night to have their teeth pulled. I never saw so many people relieved and happy to have their teeth pulled, freed from miserable pain. Can you imagine being so desperate you wanted to walk all night to get your teeth pulled? It was heartbreaking.

Since I wasn't old enough to directly help the dentists, I took on the enjoyable job of entertaining and playing with the village's children to keep them from getting in the way of the dentists. They loved seeing many of the conveniences that I had grown accustomed to, especially the video camera. I could record them and play it back. Because most of the kids did not have a mirror, this was one of the rare times they saw themselves, and they could not get enough of it. At times, dozens of kids swarmed me.

Despite seeing this poverty and providing service, I was still primarily concerned about number one. I complained about the food: rice, beans, plantains. When I worked, I tried my best not to make myself too uncomfortable or dirty. Additionally, I was focused on only doing the tasks that interested me, not necessarily what my team needed me to do. This got me into trouble as I macheted my way into a hornet's nest and got stung over ten times on my face, neck, and arms.

However, during our last couple of days in the village, my mindset shifted to outward. While I was unconscious to this change, I started to act differently, complaining less, and working harder. Instead of always wanting to be entertained, I felt the desire to uplift and serve the people in the community. I stopped defining my life by what I didn't have and started feeling grateful for the many comforts I was able to enjoy that the locals were not, like clean running water and shoes. In fact, felt stupid for the times I argued with my parents about not getting presents for Christmas that year and for always having to settle for non-name-brand clothes.

When the last day came, while I was ready for a real shower and bed, my heart was simultaneously open toward and breaking for the people we were serving. I was desperate to help them in any way we could. In many ways, we all were.

What a difference a few days makes!

I was now willing—rather *wanting*—to leave the Guatemalan villagers with as much of my clothes and stuff as I possibly could.

Never in my young life had I seen others so clearly as people with needs and feelings as important, if not more important, than my own. Never had I come to empathize with others like I did with the people in that village. While I didn't recognize this as a mindset change, it did give me a glimpse of what life could be like looking through a different lens.

I wish I could say the outward mindset stuck from that point on, but that was not the case. But since I have been working on upgrading my mindsets, this experience in the mountains of Guatemala has given me clarity on the mindset that I need to put on and wear.

The Hat

A few years ago, I had a small but meaningful experience that brought up the extreme outward feelings I experienced in Guatemala.

Every year, the Anaheim Angels partner with CSUF (home of the Titans) for Titan Night. Faculty and employees who purchase tickets and attend the game receive an Anaheim Angels hat in CSUF's colors. Wanting the hat but not finding anyone to go to the game with me, I went by myself.

One of the benefits of going to a baseball game alone is that you can usually sneak down into an unused prime seat. For much of the first seven innings, I sat only a few rows back from the Angels dugout, proudly wearing my new Angels/CSUF hat. Unfortunately, the Angels were getting clobbered. So, during the seventh-inning stretch, I started making my way up to the nearest portal to exit the stadium. As I got to the last row, a family stopped me and asked where I purchased my hat. They explained that their son (who was off buying concessions) desperately wanted a hat like mine and asked if they knew where they could purchase one. I told them I had received it as a promotional item.

Suddenly, a thought occurred to me: *Give the kid my hat!* In a quick reaction, my inward mindset immediately kicked in, reminding me this hat was the reason I had come to the game, by myself, and sat through several innings of the Angels getting creamed.

The family thanked me, and I started to walk away. For the next 50 or so steps, a debate raged in my head between the inward mindset that had arisen so strongly in that moment and my desired outward mindset. I played out all of the reasons why I was justified in keeping the hat, while my outward mindset desperately tried to ward off these justifications. But then, I asked myself a question: *How would that boy feel if I gave him the hat?* The question brought me directly into his feelings and those of his family, away from my own.

I stopped in my tracks and walked back to the family, and I gave them the hat. To my surprise, all ten of them stood up and either shook my hand or gave me a hug.

As I walked away, the feelings from Guatemala came rushing back. I knew that I had done the right thing. My outward mindset knew that the feeling of seeing and valuing others as people and giving was worth any amount of time and money.

You Can Put on an Outward Mindset

I share these experiences to demonstrate two things: first, it is possible to change our mindset from inward to outward, even for someone naturally inclined to an inward mindset, and second, life takes on incredible value when lived through an outward mindset.

Making this change isn't unique to me. Let's investigate how the leadership team of Raytheon, a large defense contractor, was able to shift from an inward to outward mindset to turn around their organization. This example comes from *The Outward Mindset*, by the Arbinger Institute.

After a corporate merger, Louise Francesconi found herself atop Raytheon Missile Systems with a directive to cut $100 million in costs within 30 days. She organized a meeting with the leaders of the different divisions to find where they could collectively cut $100 million out of their budget.

Imagine being one of the division heads coming into that meeting. What would your mindset likely be, knowing the objective and what would be required of you? You'd be protective of every budget dollar, right? Not surprisingly, these division heads carried inward mindsets, highly motivated to protect their divisions as much as possible and seeing the other division heads as competitors for precious resources.

While each division head offered perfunctory cuts, they collectively fell far short of $100 million. The discussion quickly escalated to layoffs, which led them to take on an even stronger inward mindset, practically going into bunker mentality to protect their people.

Seeing that the meeting was not going well, Francesconi did two things to alter the mindset in the room. First, on the topic of layoffs, she asked division heads to start listing the names of people who would likely be laid off. She then asked what being laid off would mean to each of those people, their families, and the larger community. These questions opened up the leaders to the fact they were not talking about objects but about people.

Second, Francesconi asked the leadership group to pair up. They spent the next two hours in one-on-one meetings with each other. In these meetings, they learned as much as they could about the other person's area of business and considered what efficiencies they could create by working together. This activity got the leadership group to stop trying to protect themselves and to start seeing the other division heads as people, whose needs and feelings were just as important as their own.

This shift in mindset resulted in amazing results. For example, one division head volunteered to fold his department into his colleague's, saving the organization $7 million while effectively lowering his position in the organizational hierarchy. Other changes of this scale occurred, too. Ultimately, by focusing on mindsets and helping divisional heads change their mindsets from being inward to outward, the leadership team cut the full $100 million from the budget, keeping layoffs at a minimum. This experience and a continued focus on having an outward mindset allowed Raytheon to double its business at a time when experts thought it couldn't grow more than 5%.

Developing an Outward Mindset

If you want to grow from an inward to an outward mindset, or simply upgrade to become even more outward minded, what can you do?

We have already covered the first half of the battle: an initial awakening process, learning about these mindsets and their powerful and diverging implications, identifying your current mindset, and remembering the memorable times you have possessed an outward mindset. The second half of the battle is changing the wiring in your brain and getting out of the rut you have likely been stuck in. To do this, we need to engage in three additional steps:

1. Recognize the cause of your inward-mindedness.
2. Consistently assess your mindset using key questions.
3. Effectively manage your self-care.

Recognize the Cause of Your Inward-Mindedness

There are two primary reasons why we turn inward: fear and self-betrayal. Until we recognize these in us, we will continue to be blind to our inwardness.

Fear

Like all negative mindsets discussed in this book, an inward mindset is rooted in fear. The specific fears that fuel an inward mindset include the following:

- Fear that there isn't enough to go around
- Fear of being passed up
- Fear of not living up to goals or expectations

When we have these fears, we are inclined to self-protect and turn inward, caring more about ourselves than others.

All three fears are also rooted in a form of deficit thinking, which I discussed in Chapter 18. When we engage in deficit thinking, we see the rewards of life (e.g., getting promoted, making money, being loved) as a fixed pie, a competition to capture as much of the pie as possible. When we see others capture significant pieces of the pie, we feel that reduces the amount of pie left to capture, driving us further inward.

During a recent conversation, a mid-level manager at a medium-sized bank explained that her gung-ho CEO had recently set a lofty goal with shareholders to double the amount of assets under management within a specific timeframe. As the deadline was nearing, she said he was growing more frantic and putting increasing pressure on the leaders and managers within the bank. She felt he was cracking the figurative whip to enhance their rate of growth.

From this woman's perspective, the CEO harbored all three of these fears. First, this goal was framed in terms of competing against other banks for customers, suggesting that there isn't enough to go around. Second, while she is not certain why the CEO set such a goal and its time frame, she suspects it is because he wanted to sell the bank, make a lot of money, and become a high-ranking official at a larger bank. This is possibly the CEO's best chance to "get ahead," and if he doesn't take advantage of it, he will "miss out" and get passed up. Third, because of the promises he made to shareholders, he surely has a fear of not living up to the goal set and shareholders' expectations.

The only way anyone is going to crack the whip is if they are unable to see those they are whipping as being a person of value. Unfortunately, because of this CEO's fears, he is operating in an inward self-protection mode. In his mind, the best way to reach the goal is to squeeze effort out of his employees, justifying his harsh and unreasonable treatment of employees. He is unable to see that doubling the bank's assets in such a short period is unlikely to occur simply as a result of the employees working harder and longer. It is likely going to require that the bank operate differently, more creatively and innovatively, than in the past. But, does cracking the whip lead to a creative and innovative environment? No, just the opposite.

His fears and inward mindset are causing him to lead and motivate in a way that is actually putting a cap on the progress the bank can make toward the goal.

In order for the CEO to find a path out, he would need to awaken to his fears and engage in abundance thinking, believing that the pie is expandable. If he believed there is enough to go around, that selling the bank isn't his one and only shot to "get ahead," and that meaningful progress toward his goal is itself a win, he would value his people more and be able to better create the innovative and creative environment required to accomplish the goal he set in the first place.

Self-Betrayal

Another reason why we turn inward is self-betrayal. Self-betrayal occurs when we get the feeling we should do something for another, and then we betray that feeling.

This seems like a small thing, and it may even be ordinary and commonplace, making it seem normal, but the implications are startling. Such betrayal can wreak emotional havoc. There is a fantastic book on self-betrayal called *Bonds that Make Us Free* by C. Terry Warner. The following example comes from this book.

Richard is in his early 30s, is married, and has a young baby. Early one morning at 2 a.m., Richard woke to hear the baby crying. In that moment, he had the feeling that he should get up with the child so that his wife would not be unnecessarily awakened. But Richard betrayed this feeling and chose not to get up and check on the baby. Because he failed to do something that he felt he should do, he had to deal with this dishonorable situation. He needed to justify his decision to betray himself.

Three responses always occur when we find ourselves having to justify our self-betrayal, which force us into an inward mindset. First, we think of excuses for why we didn't act considerately. In Richard's case, he had to make his inaction seem right. He thought about how his day started early and that he needed his sleep for his "important" day.

Second, we accuse others. As part of our justification, we feel we must identify reasons why the other person is not worthy of our consideration. In Richard's case, he started to search for reasons why his wife should get up with the baby, thinking, "It's her job to take care of the baby," "She can sleep in," and "She probably forgot to change the baby before putting her to bed, so it is her fault anyway."

Third, we view ourselves as the victim. Having excused ourselves and accused the other, we officially put ourselves in the victim role. We feel mistreated, when all that really happened is that we failed to do something we felt compelled to do. In Richard's case, he is now building the case for his inaction as though he would be required to submit a deposition in response to his inaction. When we see ourselves as the victims, we seek vigilantly for evidence that others are mistreating us.

These three responses are the only ways that we can feel right about not doing what we originally felt inclined to do. The consequence is the adoption of an inward mindset, in which we seek to elevate ourselves while diminishing others, something we are unlikely to do if we see them as people. According to Warner, the truth of the matter is that "We can't feel justified in withholding kindness from others unless we find, or invent, some reason why they deserve it."

Self-betrayal and our responses to it start a vicious negative cycle that destroys relationships. It starts with our own wrongdoing but ends with us believing that others have done wrong to us.

We can even play this out. How is Richard likely to treat his wife in the morning? In response, how is she likely to respond to him? Now they are in gridlock, all because Richard betrayed himself.

Awakening to Our Fear and Self-Betrayal

The two primary reasons why we turn inward, fear and self-betrayal, make it easy for us to justify possessing an inward mindset. When we are unaware of our fear and self-betrayal, we are oblivious that we even have an inward mindset and, unfortunately, blind to the fact that there is a much better and more productive alternative. Until we can awaken to the reasons why we turn inward, we will have a difficult time shifting our mindsets to be more outward.

Consistently Assess Your Mindset Using Key Questions

Improving our mindsets involves rewiring our brain. We can do this by engaging in small interventions repeated over time.

One of the best ways to rewire our brain to become more outward is to consistently evaluate our mindset by asking pointed questions, such as:

- Am I seeing others as people or as objects?
- Are they doing their best?
- Who am I being that their light is not shining?

These questions enable us to consciously reset our mindset to be more outward. The more we reset over time, the more likely we will stick with an outward mindset.

Two other introspective questions taken from *Bonds that Make Us Free* are:

- Do you love yourself in the theater or the theater in yourself?
- If you could select one of the following pictures to be on the cover of your life's book, which would it be?
  a. You surrounded by your admirers, with you as the focal point
  b. The people you love and are most concerned about

Both questions are powerful because they force us to wrestle with our priorities and how we see ourselves relative to others.

Effectively Manage Your Self-Care

If our body needs something, our mind focuses on fulfilling that need, and with this focus comes an inward mindset.

Unless we are in a truly desperate situation, the two most common needs that we encounter and can personally control are hunger and fatigue. When we become hungry or fatigued, resolving these needs becomes our primary focus. When they overcome us, it becomes easier to view people as objects and obstacles getting in the way of fulfilling our need. Hence the terms *hangry* and *cranky*. Thus, it is important to be intentional about your food, meals, rest, and sleep.

But, more broadly, effectively managing self-care means creating or finding balance in our lives. When we are out of whack, stressed, or overly emotional, we are going to feel more inclined to self-protect and focus inward, limiting our ability to reach outward to empathize with others.

Additional Resources

If you find that this set of mindsets is one that you need to work on, here are some additional sources that I have found helpful:

- *Leadership and Self-Deception, Anatomy of Peace,* and *The Outward Mindset* by the Arbinger Institute
- *Bonds that Make Us Free* by C. Terry Warner
- *Dare to Lead* by Brené Brown
- *The Shift: How Seeing People as People Changes Everything* by Kimberly White
- *The Conscious Parent: Transforming Ourselves, Empowering Our Children* by Shefali Tsabary

Summary

A common phrase used to describe a shift from an inward to outward mindset is "a change of heart." You move from a self-focused mentality, focused on protecting and advancing yourself, to opening your heart to the value and beauty of others.

This shift, or change of heart, requires that you:

1. Learn about these mindsets and their power.
2. Awaken to your current mindset.
3. Recall the times when you possessed an outward mindset, to remind you of your possibilities.
4. Investigate and recognize the cause of your inward-mindedness.
5. Consistently assess your mindset using key introspective questions.
6. Effectively manage your self-care.

PART VI
CONCLUSION

Chapter 21

SUCCESS REQUIRES GETTING
TO THE ROOT OF OUR PAIN

To heal, you have to get to the root of the wound and kiss it all the way up.

—Rupi Kaur

A few years ago, my wife became a more regular runner, generally running about 20 miles a week. While she was enjoying her new hobby, she was hampered by nagging knee pain. Her initial steps to treat the pain were similar to how I dealt with my knee pain, which I recounted in Chapter 1. She bought new shoes and had me teach her the four principles to good running form.

Unfortunately, the four principles didn't resolve her issue.

Shortly thereafter, while we were on a family vacation, we spent time with my brother, an occupational therapist. Growing impatient and increasingly frustrated, she asked him if there was anything she could do to treat this pain. He explained that because of a loose patellar tendon, her kneecap was not as stable as it should be. He suggested that she wear a knee brace.

She tried it, and it seemed to do the trick. As she continued to run with the knee brace, her pain dissipated.

Then, a series of events occurred that led to greater awareness about her knee and caused her to realize that while wearing a brace may reduce the pain, it wasn't actually addressing the problem.

These events began with my family going on a cruise. Since I was training for a half marathon, one of the first things I did after boarding the cruise ship was check out the gym. I found a number of different stations promoting health-related products for passengers. A personal trainer awaited at one of the stations. He asked me to take off my shoes and step on a white pad on the floor. I indulged him. I stepped onto the pad, which turned out to be a pressure plate designed to help me see how I distributed my weight across my foot when I stepped. Being the salesman that he was, he said my weight distribution was all off-kilter. He then proceeded to tell me about the importance of orthotics and showed me a small insert I could put into my shoe to help my posture, balance, and running form.

Until this time, I didn't know much about orthotics, although I held the stereotype that they were generally for "old people." Between that stereotype and the outrageous price point, I passed.

But shortly after we got home from the cruise, I ran with a running group. One of the members happened to be a podiatrist. So, I asked him about orthotics and if I should get some. Three other runners quickly jumped in, proclaiming the value of orthotics. It turned out that I was essentially the only person in the running group without them. The podiatrist added that he had been running with orthotics for over 30 years. He ticked off a list of the benefits of orthotics, while also dismissing some common myths that the trainer had told me on the cruise.

I worked with this podiatrist to get some orthotics. In the process, I learned that my insurance would cover the cost of the orthotics and the doctor's appointments associated with getting them.

Upon learning this, my wife set up an appointment with a podiatrist. One of the first things this podiatrist did was take an X-ray of her foot. It revealed a number of significant issues, including bowed metatarsals, unnatural spacing between her metatarsals, and a flatter midfoot than ideal. Concerned about what she was seeing on the screen, she asked the podiatrist why she had so many issues. He told her it was a combination of genetics and wearing shoes with inadequate support.

The podiatrist proceeded to tell her that the foundational cause of her knee pain was her feet. Her loose patellar tendon was the result of her leg muscles compensating for her foot problems. While a knee brace would reduce the pain she experienced while running, he said it would not get rid of the problem. He added that if she didn't address her foot problems, other issues would pop up in her legs over time.

She was blown away. For years, she had been experiencing knee pain and tried all sorts of things to resolve the issue. While thinking she had resolved the issue by getting a knee brace, she had just come to learn that her knee wasn't the problem. Instead, it was something more foundational—her feet. Had she not learned this, she would have continued to treat the pain at the surface level, where the pain appeared, and never properly treated the actual problem.

Awakening to this, she now felt much more empowered to address her pain and the issues hindering her running. She could now get to the source of the problem and root it out, and along the way prevent a whole host of other issues she would likely experience throughout her life had she not learned about her foot issues.

Foundational Role of Mindsets

Just as my wife's feet are foundational to her running experience, our mindsets are foundational to our success across our life, work, and leadership.

Are you experiencing pain or discomfort in your life, work, or leadership? This could be because things aren't going well. Or it could be because while things are good, you want better and haven't been able to make the progress that you want or expect.

Further, if you are experiencing any pain or discomfort in your life, work, or leadership, how have you treated that pain? Have you been focused on where the pain is occurring? Or have you tried to find the root of the pain and treat it there?

If we continue to be blind to our mindsets, we will misdiagnose our problems, treat them only at the surface level, and continue to be frustrated.

That was the case with Alan, the president of the nonprofit we have discussed throughout the book. He was experiencing pain in the form of frustrations with employees and low levels of employee performance. In response, he was trying to treat this pain where it was felt. To treat his frustration, he has resorted to micromanaging his employees. To treat low levels of performance, he fired them or forced them out. The results of these actions, while making sense in the moment, only served to enhance Alan's frustration. He now feels he has to monitor his employees more strictly and spend a significant amount of time hiring and bringing new employees up to speed instead of pushing the business forward.

There is one thing Alan hasn't done: consider the root source of these issues—his mindsets. Until he awakens to them, he won't be able to stop the negative cycles causing ongoing frustration and slowing his organization's progress.

Organizational Mindsets

Just as overlooking our mindsets leads to frustration and ultimately limits our progress at an individual level, it has the same consequences at an organizational level.

Think of some of the most common organizational problems:

- Poor leadership and management
- Inability to effectively initiate and navigate change
- Lack of inclusion
- Low employee morale and effectiveness

At the root of each of these issues lies negative mindsets.

In my consulting practice, I go into organizations and ask their employees, most often top leadership teams, to take my mindset assessment. This allows us to assess the collective mindsets of the organization. The results help me quickly understand the organization's culture, fears, and strengths. Then, through a discussion of these issues, I work with the organization to diagnose and specifically identify the root of their common problems and what is preventing greater success. In turn, I am able to help them treat the issue at the source, upgrading the mindsets that have been holding them back and unlocking the greater success they are seeking.

Let me give you a couple of examples.

First, I was fortunate to work with a Fortune 10 organization. They approached me because they wanted to ensure their top 130 leaders possessed the most effective mindsets prior to engaging in a large merger. This assessment revealed areas of strength and weakness. The strength of their culture was that it was an open-minded leadership group. In all, 57% of leaders had a strong open mindset, 81% were on the open mindset side of the continuum, and only 4% of leaders had a strong closed mindset. This openness would help them ensure a psychologically safe environment for the employees in the organization they were merging with.

The weakness of their leadership culture was that a significant percentage of leaders, 42%, operated with a fixed mindset. When approaching a challenge, 42% of their leaders were mentally programmed to avoid the challenge and protect their self-image rather than view the challenge as an opportunity to learn, grow, and advance—a big red flag. But, knowing that this was their biggest mindset issue, they could then do something about it, so I helped them develop initiatives to help their top leaders become more growth-minded.

Second, I had an opportunity to work with the top 40 leaders of a mid-sized customer service company. The results of the assessment were much less positive. About 50% of leaders held a fixed mindset, 48% a closed mindset, 66% a prevention mindset, and 34% an inward mindset.

As we discussed these results, we uncovered a lot of fear in the organization, mostly a fear of failure. What leaders and employees alike had experienced is that if they make mistakes with clients, their clients will leave and find another vendor. So, the organization's leaders largely created a fear of failure. While their fear was well-intended, I was able to help them see that it bore some ugly side effects, both internally and externally. Internally, it meant that employees didn't feel safe to make mistakes. This carries two major negative implications: it stifles creativity and innovation, and when mistakes and problems actually occur, employees try their hardest to cover them up rather than bring them to light to properly address and avoid them in the future. Externally, it meant that while the company might not be displeasing clients, they likely weren't pleasing them, either. The absence of problems does not mean satisfaction.

Additionally, when we looked across the top 40 leaders, we found that 66% carried at least two negative mindsets, of which 29% possessed at least three negative mindsets, and 13% operated with all four of the negative mindsets. If you were to enter this organization, it isn't likely that you will be managed in a very effective way. The majority of the organization's leaders possessed mindsets that limit success, disengage employees, and cause frustration. Collectively, these results indicated that the culture is one where leaders and employees are more focused on self-protecting than advancing the organization.

When comparing these two organizations, it is easy for me to see which company enjoys better leadership and management, is going to initiate and navigate change more effectively, is more inclusive, and has higher employee morale and effectiveness.

Regardless of which organization has the better mindset foundation at the moment, the value of assessing the collective mindset of each organization's leaders was the same. The leaders were able to enhance their self-awareness by awakening to their mindsets, identifying the root cause of their common pains, frustrations, and overall lack of progress; and being empowered to resolve their issues at their foundational level.

Awakening to Our Mindsets

Thousands of people have taken the personal mindset assessment associated with this book. I have found that only 5% of them consistently utilize and operate with the mindsets necessary for success.

If you are one of the 95% with some room to improve your mindsets, welcome to the club! This is where I reside. Our lives, the contexts we find ourselves in, and our often misguided best efforts have led us to unintentionally develop mindsets that are putting a cap on our success.

Do not feel defeated. Possessing less-than-ideal mindsets is no fault of our own. We have unknowingly underestimated the power and importance of mindsets and lacked a language and framework to be able to identify our current mindsets, the mindsets most conducive to success, and our path to a brighter and more successful future.

I wake up every day with great hope that my efforts to improve my mental lenses will result in new and previously unseen levels of performance and success. I hope you feel the same way. To that end, I offer you a whole series of hopes:

- I hope that from reading this book, you have awakened to the foundational and crucial role mindsets play in your life.
- I hope you now can move forward with a language and framework to talk about and evaluate your mindsets.
- I hope you are now able to identify the mindsets most conducive to success, and that through the examples and research presented in this book, you see the power in the four Success Mindsets that it promotes.
- I hope you are able to see just how important each Success Mindset is. What happens if even one mindset, or part of a mindset, is off? Do you get a sense of how that limits you?
- I hope you have been able to assess your current mindsets and where they fall on the negative-to-positive continuum.
- I hope this book has provided some guidance on how to upgrade your mindsets to unlock greater success in your life, work, and leadership.

Ultimately, I hope you feel both liberated and empowered. When we are not conscious of the foundational role mindsets play in our lives and the specific mindsets we possess, we become enslaved by the negative aspects of our mindsets. Now that you have awakened to your mindsets, I hope you feel empowered to loosen the bonds that have been holding you back, and I hope you feel empowered to rise to new heights.

At different points in my life, I have operated on the negative side of each of the four mindset continuums. As I experienced this awakening process for myself, I felt liberated and empowered. While my mindsets aren't always ideal, I do largely operate on the positive side of each of the continuums today. Before making these upgrades, progress felt about as easy as pushing a car through mud.

With these upgrades, progress comes much more smoothly. I feel like a well-oiled sports car.

Regardless of where your mindsets currently stand, you are way ahead of the curve. Think for a moment: what percentage of your friends, colleagues, and family members know what you now know about mindsets? Essentially everyone is blind to their power, and even fewer know the specific mindsets they need to possess to unlock greater success in their life, work, and leadership. You no longer need to hunt in the dark, hoping you stumble across the keys of success. You have been handed those keys. Now, the question is: What will you do with them?

While we end this exploration of mindsets here, it is not the end of the story. The real story is what you do with the awakening you have experienced and the keys you have been given. What is there that you *can't* do if you develop the four Success Mindsets? You can do almost anything; question is: *Will you?* I hope that because of what you have learned and applied from this book, people will write books about you and the story you live.

Now go and create it.

Be growth-minded: believe that you and others can change abilities, talents, and intelligence.

Be open-minded: seek after truth and optimal thinking.

Be promotion-minded: have a clear purpose and destination that you are shooting toward.

Be outward-minded: see others as people of great worth and value them as such.

Now, go out and change the world with your new mindsets!

ABOUT THE AUTHOR

Ryan Gottfredson, PhD,, is a mental success coach and cutting-edge leadership consultant, author, trainer, and researcher. He helps improve organizations, leaders, teams, and employees by improving their mindsets. Ryan is currently a leadership and management professor at the Mihaylo College of Business and Economics at California State University, Fullerton. He holds a PhD in Organizational Behavior and Human Resources from Indiana University and a BA from Brigham Young University. He is also a former consultant for Gallup, Inc., where he helped dozens of organizations improve the engagement of their employees. As a respected authority and researcher on topics related to leadership, management, and organizational behavior, Ryan has published over 15 articles in a variety of journals, including *Journal of Management, Journal of Organizational Behavior, Business Horizons, Journal of Leadership and Organizational Studies*, and *Journal of Leadership Studies*. His research has been cited over 1,700 times since 2014. Connect with Ryan at https://www.ryangottfredson.com.

CPSIA information can be obtained
at www.ICGtesting.com
Printed in the USA
BVHW031434241219
567672BV00003B/15/P